Original title: Horse Racing. Secrets and Curiosities

© Horse Racing. Secrets and Curiosities, Carlos Martínez Cerdá and Víctor Martínez Cerdá, 2024

Authors: Víctor Martínez Cerdá and Carlos Martínez Cerdá (V&C Brothers)

© Cover and illustrations: V&C Brothers

Layout and design: V&C Brothers

All rights reserved.

This publication may not be reproduced, stored, recorded, or transmitted in any form or by any means, whether mechanical, photochemical, electronic, magnetic, electro-optical, by photocopying, or information retrieval systems, or any other current or future method, without prior written permission from the copyright holders.

# HORSE RACING

Secrets and Curiosities

# 1

## Countries with the most followers.

**1. Japan:** Japan is one of the countries with the largest number of horse racing fans. The sport is extremely popular, with events like the Japan Cup and the Tokyo Yushun (Japanese Derby) drawing huge crowds. It is estimated that more than 13 million people in Japan actively follow horse racing. Additionally, betting on horse races is an important part of the country's sports culture, generating billions of dollars in revenue each year.

**2. United States:** Home to the Triple Crown (comprised of the Kentucky Derby, the Preakness Stakes, and the Belmont Stakes), the United States has a large and devoted fan base. More than 10 million people follow horse racing in the country, and major events generate enormous interest. Betting on horse races is also a key part of the culture, with several states legalizing sports betting to support the industry.

**3. United Kingdom:** With a horse racing tradition that dates back centuries, the United Kingdom is another country with millions of followers. Events like the Royal Ascot, the Grand National, and the 2000 Guineas are of great significance. It is estimated that around 6 million people in the UK actively follow horse racing. Additionally, betting on horse races is a cornerstone of the British betting industry, which has significantly contributed to the sport's popularity.

**4. Australia:** Horse racing in Australia is deeply rooted in the country's culture, with events like the Melbourne Cup attracting millions of viewers each year.

It is estimated that more than 5 million people actively follow horse racing in Australia. The Melbourne Cup, known as "the race that stops a nation," is practically a national holiday.

**5. Hong Kong:** Despite its relatively small size, Hong Kong is one of the world's most important centers for horse racing. The Sha Tin and Happy Valley racecourses are famous for their large crowds and high-level events. Around 2.5 million people follow horse racing in Hong Kong, and betting is incredibly popular, with one of the most lucrative horse racing industries in the world.

**6. France:** France has a rich horse racing tradition, with events like the Prix de l'Arc de Triomphe, one of the most prestigious races in the world. It is estimated that around 3 million people in France follow horse racing. The country also has a long history of thoroughbred breeding and a well-developed horse racing industry.

**7. Ireland:** Ireland has a strong heritage in horse racing, both in breeding and organizing events. The Irish Derby and the Punchestown Festival are just a few examples of events that attract many fans. Approximately 2 million people in Ireland are active horse racing fans, and thoroughbred breeding is an important part of the country's economy.

**8. Argentina:** Argentina has a deep connection to horse racing, with events like the Gran Premio Carlos Pellegrini drawing considerable crowds. It is estimated that around 1.5 million people in Argentina are active horse racing fans, and the country has produced some of the best horses and jockeys in history.

**9. South Africa:** Horse racing is a major sport, with events like the Durban July and the Sun Met attracting large crowds. It is estimated that around 1 million people actively follow horse racing in the country.

**10. United Arab Emirates (UAE):** In the UAE, particularly in Dubai, horse racing has grown exponentially in popularity, especially with events like the Dubai World Cup, one of the most lucrative races in the world. It is estimated that around 800,000 people in the Emirates are horse racing enthusiasts, with the event drawing international fans, world-class jockeys, and horse owners.

**11. New Zealand:** New Zealand has a long tradition in horse racing, both in terms of horse breeding and hosting major events. The New Zealand Derby and the New Zealand Cup are standout events on the country's racing calendar. It is estimated that around 700,000 people actively follow horse racing in New Zealand. Additionally, the country has produced some of the most successful horses and jockeys on the international stage.

**12. Brazil:** Brazil is another Latin American country with a strong following for horse racing. The Grande Prêmio Brasil is the country's most important event, held at the Hipódromo da Gávea in Rio de Janeiro. Approximately 500,000 people actively follow horse racing in Brazil, and the sport continues to grow.

**13. Italy:** Italy has a rich horse racing tradition, with events like the Gran Premio di Milano and the historic Palio di Siena, which attracts thousands of spectators. It is estimated that around 400,000 people follow horse racing in Italy, where horse breeding has also been a significant activity.

# 2

## Superstitions of famous jockeys.

**-Lester Piggott:** The legendary British jockey was very superstitious and never allowed anyone to wish him "good luck" before a race. He believed that wishing luck brought bad fortune, so he preferred that no one say anything to him before heading to the racetrack.

**-Frankie Dettori:** One of the most famous jockeys in the world, he never walks under a ladder before a race, as he considers it bad luck. He also has the superstition of kissing his horse on the nose before mounting it.

**-Bill Shoemaker:** This famous American jockey never allowed anyone to touch his helmet or boots before a race. He believed that if someone did, it would bring him bad luck.

**-Willie Shoemaker:** The legendary jockey had a superstition related to numbers. He preferred to wear the number 3 on his jersey whenever possible, as he considered it his lucky number.

**-Pat Day:** This American jockey always said a brief prayer before each race, asking for protection and success, a ritual he maintained throughout his career.

**-Johnny Murtagh:** The Irish jockey is known for his belief in the importance of wearing the same pair of gloves in consecutive races if he had won previously. If he won a race, he would continue to wear those gloves until he lost a race.

**-John Velazquez:** The Puerto Rican jockey never wore yellow clothing, as he believed that the color brought bad luck in races.

He avoided anything related to that color, from clothing to horse equipment.

**-Ruby Walsh:** Famous jump jockey Ruby Walsh never mounts his horse by putting his left foot in the stirrup first. He always starts with his right foot, believing that this protects him from falls and accidents.

**-Javier Castellano:** This Venezuelan jockey made sure not o step on the white lines painted on the track before a race. He believed that stepping on the lines would bring bad luck and affect his performance.

**-Ryan Moore:** The British jockey avoids saying or hearing the word "lose" before a race. Any mention of defeat or failure is, for him, a bad omen, so he avoids that conversation in the minutes leading up to a race.

**-Kieren Fallon:** The famous Irish jockey had a specific ritual: he always placed his left stirrup on the horse first, without exception, believing that this would bring him good luck and balance during the race.

**-Mike Smith:** This American jockey always prayed silently before mounting his horse. This ritual was not only a way to ask for success but also to calm his nerves before the race.

**-Garrett Gomez:** The late American jockey had the superstition of not changing his goggles between races if he had won. He believed that changing his goggles after a victory would break his "winning streak."

**-Eddie Arcaro:** Famous American jockey who won the Kentucky Derby five times, Arcaro always carried a small lucky coin in his pocket during races. He believed it brought him good fortune at critical moments.

**-Victor Espinoza:** The Mexican jockey, known for winning the Triple Crown with American Pharoah, always rides his horse using the same helmet and jacket if he has won a major race. He only changes his gear when he loses, believing that keeping the same equipment maintains good energy.

**-Angel Cordero Jr.:** The legendary Puerto Rican jockey avoided wearing green clothing or gear. He considered green to be a color that brought bad luck in races and always ensured that he wore nothing of that color during competitions.

**-Gary Stevens:** This American jockey used to carry a lucky charm in the form of a stone, given to him by a close friend. He always kept it in his pocket during important races to attract good fortune.

**-Christophe Soumillon:** The Belgian jockey never looked back during a race, as he believed doing so brought bad luck and could affect his concentration. Keeping his eyes forward was, according to him, key to his success.

**-Jerry Bailey:** Before every race, Bailey had the habit of mounting his horse from the left side. Although this is common practice in equestrian traditions, Bailey considered it an essential ritual to ensure a good performance.

**-Richard Hughes:** The Irish jockey had a superstition related to weights. He always checked his weight twice before a race to ensure everything was in order, believing that failing to do so could affect his performance.

# 3

## Famous quotes.

### 1. Lester Piggott:

- "Hard work always beats talent when talent doesn't work hard."
- "It's a game of patience and control, not just speed."
- "Every race is a new opportunity to win, never take it for granted."

### 2. Frankie Dettori:

- "It doesn't matter how many times you win, each victory is as sweet as the first."
- "Winning is thrilling, but the true magic lies in the relationship with the horse."
- "The moment before the race is when everything stops, and only the horse and I matter."

### 3. Willie Shoemaker:

- "The secret is keeping your horse balanced and not letting it lose its stride."
- "Riding a horse is like dancing, it's all about rhythm and grace."
- "Size doesn't matter when you have the heart of a champion."

### 4. Angel Cordero Jr.:

- "No matter how fast your horse runs, the most important thing is how much it wants to win."
- "A good jockey must feel what the horse needs, not just direct it."
- "Confidence in your horse is half the victory."

## 5. Pat Day:

- "You always have to ride with faith, not with fear."
- "Riding horses teaches you more about yourself than anything else."
- "Success is the result of patience and preparation."

## 6. Mike Smith:

- "Being a jockey is about confidence in yourself and the horse you're riding."
- "Every horse has its own rhythm, your job is to find it."
- "It's not just about speed, it's knowing when to push and when to ease off."

## 7. Gary Stevens:

- "Anything can happen in racing, and it often does."
- "Victory is sweet, but perseverance is what gets you there."
- "You have to ride as if every race is your last."

## 8. Jerry Bailey:

- "You have to listen to your horse. They tell you what they need, and you have to be willing to listen."
- "The real secret is in knowing your horse's heart."
- "The best jockey is the one who adapts to the horse, not the other way around."

## 9. Kent Desormeaux:

- "There's no better feeling than crossing the finish line first."
- "The bond with your horse is what leads you to victory."
- "Every race is different, but the goal is always the same: to win."

## 10. Victor Espinoza:

- "Victory is always a special moment, but preparation is what makes it possible."

- "Success is a team effort between the horse and the jockey."
- "You can never be confident in a race until you cross the finish line."

## 11. Christophe Soumillon:

- "Patience is as important as speed in a race."
- "Riding is an art, not a science."
- "The horse feels your energy, which is why it's key to stay calm before every race."

## 12. Ryan Moore:

- "Horses don't understand betting. They only know how to run."
- "Every horse is unique, and every race requires a different strategy."
- "The most important thing is always being in the right place at the right time."

## 13. Javier Castellano:

- "You have to be in sync with the horse to win, you can't force anything."
- "A good jockey adapts to the horse, not the other way around."
- "The key to success lies in the details others overlook."

## 14. John Velazquez:

- "Success in racing is not just talent, it's also strategy and discipline."
- "Confidence is what makes the difference between winning and losing."
- "Riding horses is a blend of technique, instinct, and heart."

## 15. Richard Hughes:

- "The key is finding the perfect balance between control and the horse's freedom."

- "A good jockey knows when to let the horse run free."
- "Every victory is a reward for the invisible effort behind the scenes."

## 16. Kieren Fallon:

- "Success doesn't come easily. Every victory requires sacrifice and dedication."
- "Confidence in the horse is just as important as technique."
- "Never underestimate the power of a horse to surprise you."

## 17. Garrett Gomez:

- "It's more than speed, it's having control at all times."
- "Riding a horse is like telling a story: it has a beginning, a middle, and an end."
- "You should always have a plan, but be ready to improvise."

## 18. Ruby Walsh:

- "It's not about winning every time, but about winning the ones that matter."
- "The horse takes you to the limit, but you decide whether to cross the line."
- "Perseverance is the only way to get through the tough days."

## 19. Bill Shoemaker:

- "It's not the size of the jockey that matters, but the will to win."
- "Riding horses is more than technique, it's intuition and connection."

# 4

**Elite horse racing trainers.**

**1. Bob Baffert:** He is arguably one of the most recognized trainers in modern horse racing history. Baffert has won the Kentucky Derby multiple times, including with legendary horses like American Pharoah and Justify, both Triple Crown winners. In 2015, American Pharoah ended a 37-year drought without a Triple Crown winner, and Justify repeated the feat in 2018. Baffert is known for his ability to train horses for major events and his meticulous attention to detail in every aspect of training.

**2. Aidan O'Brien, from Ireland:** He is another elite trainer in the world of horse racing. O'Brien has trained some of the best horses in the history of European racing, including winners of the Epsom Derby, the Prix de l'Arc de Triomphe, and many other major events. Primarily working for Coolmore Stud, one of the world's leading horse breeding operations, he has won numerous British Classics and set a record by training 28 Group 1 winners in a single season.

**3. Todd Pletcher:** He is one of the most successful trainers in the United States. He has won the Kentucky Derby, the Belmont Stakes, and multiple Eclipse Awards for Trainer of the Year. Pletcher is known for his methodical and careful approach to training horses. He has produced champion horses in all the major Triple Crown races and has maintained remarkable consistency over the years, making him one of the most respected trainers in the North American racing circuit.

**4. John Gosden:** A highly esteemed British trainer, known for his success in both Europe and the United States. He has trained winners of the Epsom Derby, the King George VI and Queen Elizabeth Stakes, and the Prix de l'Arc de Triomphe.

Horses like Enable and Stradivarius have been great champions under his guidance. Gosden is a master at preparing horses for long-distance events and is known for his exceptional ability to understand the personality and needs of each of his horses.

**5. André Fabre:** One of the great European trainers, specifically from France. Throughout his career, he has won the prestigious Prix de l'Arc de Triomphe multiple times, Europe's most important race. He is known for his meticulous approach and his ability to prepare horses for major international competitions. Fabre has worked with some of the most influential owners in the world and has trained world-class horses for decades.

**6. D. Wayne Lukas:** A pioneer in horse training in the United States, with a career spanning more than four decades. Lukas has won the Kentucky Derby four times and has multiple victories in the Belmont Stakes and the Preakness Stakes. He is known for revolutionizing modern training in the U.S. and was the first to adopt a more corporate team structure, with assistant trainers and a strong focus on statistics.

**7. Charlie Appleby:** Another highly successful British trainer, working for Godolphin, the racing operation of Sheikh Mohammed bin Rashid Al Maktoum. Appleby has won major races around the world, including the Epsom Derby and the Breeders' Cup in the United States. Appleby has elevated Godolphin to new heights with his innovative strategies and his ability to prepare horses for major competitions on multiple continents.

**8. Mark Casse:** Known for his success in both the United States and Canada, having won the Queen's Plate and multiple U.S. Triple Crown races. Casse has been a key figure in North American horse racing and has won Eclipse Awards, as well as being inducted into the Saratoga Race Course Hall of Fame. His approach has brought fame to horses like Tepin and War of Will.

**9. Saeed bin Suroor:** One of the leading trainers for Godolphin, he has had considerable success in Europe, the United States, and the Middle East. Under his guidance, Godolphin has won several of the most prestigious races in the world, including the Dubai World Cup, one of the richest races globally. Saeed bin Suroor has been a consistent figure in international racing, achieving multiple Group 1 victories.

**10. Michael Stoute:** One of the longest-standing and most successful trainers in the United Kingdom, with multiple victories in major races such as the Epsom Derby and the King George VI and Queen Elizabeth Stakes. Stoute is known for his patient approach and for getting his horses to peak at the right time. He has trained champions like Shergar and Pilsudski and remains a prominent figure in the racing world.

# 5

**The ancient origins of horse racing date back to very early times, and its practice is deeply rooted in the history of human civilizations.**

From the moment humans began to domesticate horses, competitions involving the speed and endurance of these animals naturally began to emerge.

The earliest written references to horse racing come from ancient Mesopotamia and Egypt, where races were held as part of religious celebrations and social events.

However, it was in ancient Greece and Rome that these races became institutionalized as a sport and a popular form of entertainment.

In Ancient Greece, horse racing, particularly chariot racing, was already a part of the ancient Olympic Games.

In 648 BC, during the XXXIII Olympic Games, chariot races were included for the first time in the official program of the Olympic competitions.

These races were held in the Hippodrome of Olympia, a specific venue designed to host horse racing and other equestrian competitions.

The inclusion of chariot races marked an important point in the evolution of the sport, as it not only involved the skill and dexterity of the charioteer (the driver of the chariot), but also the endurance and speed of the horses.

These competitions were extremely violent and dangerous,

both for the horses and the drivers, often ending in catastrophic accidents.

In the Olympic races, quadrigas (chariots drawn by four horses) were the most popular type of competition, although there were also other variants with chariots drawn by two horses (bigas).

These races symbolized not only the physical prowess of the horses but also the status and prestige of the race team owners, who were often members of the aristocracy.

The charioteers who won these competitions received great honors, and the horses were also treated with almost divine respect, sometimes even being consecrated to the gods.

During Ancient Rome, horse racing gained even more importance, becoming one of the main mass spectacles of the Roman Empire.

In this culture, the quadriga races, held in large venues like the Circus Maximus, were the main attraction for the Roman people.

These races, according to Roman legends dating back to the times of Romulus and Remus, were seen as a symbol of Rome's military strength and power.

Initially, the quadrigas were pulled by mules, but they were later replaced by horses, which brought greater speed and spectacle to the competitions.

Horses, easier to tame and faster than mules, allowed the races to become more exciting and visually appealing.

The Circus Maximus, with a capacity of over 250,000

spectators, became the epicenter of this type of entertainment in Rome.

The chariot races were events filled with excitement and danger. The charioteers raced at breakneck speeds around the circus, and collisions were common, adding to the spectacle for the audience.

The factions or racing teams (identified by the colors they represented, such as red, blue, green, and white) had fanatical followers, and the rivalry between them was fierce.

Throughout the Roman Empire, chariot racing came to symbolize public entertainment par excellence and became one of the central forms of celebration during Roman festivals and festivities.

One of the most notable aspects of chariot racing in Rome was its role as a social and political meeting point.

Emperors and political leaders often used these events to gain public favor by sponsoring races and awarding generous prizes to the winners.

This sport not only provided entertainment but also served as a way to control and appease the people during times of social tension.

Chariot racing also inspired the creation of architectural complexes like the circuses, massive structures specifically designed to host these competitions.

The Circus Maximus was the largest of all, but there were other important circuses, such as the Circus Flaminius and the Circus of Nero.

These venues became the epicenter of social life in Rome, and the public flocked to watch the competitions and support their favorite teams.

With the fall of the Roman Empire, chariot racing and the culture of the circuses began to lose significance and gradually fell out of use.

Although they were no longer the main form of entertainment, horse racing did not disappear entirely.

# 6

**The modern origin of horse racing as we know it today has its roots in 12th-century Europe.**

During this period, various horse breeds began to be crossbred with the aim of improving their characteristics, seeking animals with both endurance and speed.

These crossbreeds were especially common in England, where Arabian and Barb horses were brought to be bred with the native horses of the British Isles.

These mixes gave rise to the thoroughbred, one of the fastest and most elegant horse breeds in the world.

A key moment in the development of horse racing came in 1174, when King Charles II of England, a sports enthusiast, organized one of the first official horse competitions in Europe.

The king, known for his love of entertainment and competition, promoted this sport among the nobility and aristocracy.

During his reign, horse racing began to gain popularity among the British elite, becoming a symbol of prestige and status.

The true rise of professional horse racing occurred in the 18th century, specifically between 1702 and 1714, under the reign of Queen Anne of England.

During her rule, horse racing was formalized and established as an official sport, with more structured and regular events.

Queen Anne actively promoted horse racing, and under her patronage, these competitions became more organized, with clear rules and substantial prizes.

This marked the beginning of horse racing as we know it today, with jockeys, trained horses, and betting.

A key point in the history of horse racing was the development of the town of Newmarket, which became the epicenter of the horse racing world in England.

Newmarket, which had been a racing center since the 1600s, was formalized as the location for the country's most important competitions.

During this time, specific rules were introduced, such as the requirement that horses must carry a weight of 63 kg to compete, in order to ensure fairness in the competitions.

At Newmarket, the nobility and the horse racing elite gathered to compete and socialize, establishing standards for future horse races.

It was here that the idea was solidified that horse racing was not just entertainment, but also a social and economic activity of great importance.

The introduction of rules and regulations regarding weight, race distances, and horse breeding helped formalize and professionalize the sport, which until then had primarily been a pastime for the nobility.

The birth of the English thoroughbred is also tied to this period in history.

Thoroughbreds are the result of crossbreeding Arabian, Turkoman, and Barb horses with English mares.

These horses were bred specifically to be fast, agile, and strong, essential traits for competing in speed races.

The three most important stallions from which all modern thoroughbreds descend are Byerley Turk, Darley Arabian, and Godolphin Arabian.

These imported horses brought a mix of genes that, when crossed with English horses, gave rise to the thoroughbred breed as we know it today.

Throughout the 18th and 19th centuries, horse racing continued to evolve and expand beyond England.

France and the United States also embraced the sport with enthusiasm, and races began to be held in many other countries.

During this time, the rules and formats of races became standardized, and betting became an integral part of the sport.

Betting on horse races, in particular, helped make the sport more accessible to a broader audience, not just the aristocracy, which increased its popularity among all social classes.

In addition to the competitions themselves, horse racing became a lucrative industry, driving horse breeding, betting, and tourism.

Racetracks were built around the world, and horse racing became one of the most popular and widely followed sports, not only in Europe but also in America, Australia, and other continents.

The races at Newmarket laid the foundation for other major

competitions, and today, events like the Epsom Derby, which began in 1780, and the 2000 Guineas trace their origins back to this period of growth and development in the sport.

Horse racing became firmly established as an important tradition in British and European culture, with clear rules, meticulously trained horses, and highly skilled jockeys.

# 7

**In the modern Olympic Games, equestrian events made their first appearance in the second edition, held in 1900 in Paris.**

It was during these Games that equestrian sports were included for the first time as an Olympic event, featuring jumping and endurance competitions.

However, in this initial participation, the format and rules were quite different from what we know today, and equestrian sports were not part of the official program in the following Olympics. They were permanently reintroduced in 1912.

During the 1900 Paris Olympics, equestrian competitions were divided into jumping events and military equestrian trials.

There were events for both civilian and military horses and riders, reflecting the fundamental role horses played in society at the time, both in the military and in everyday life.

Horses were a crucial part of transportation and the military, and this was reflected in the early inclusion of equestrian sports in the Olympic Games.

In the first edition of Olympic equestrian events, the most prominent trials included show jumping, which became one of the sport's most iconic disciplines.

Riders had to guide their horses over a series of obstacles, and the competition was judged based on the height and distance of the jumps, as well as the elegance and control of the rider over the horse.

This first Olympic show jumping competition was won by a

Belgian military officer named Aimé Haegeman, riding a horse named Benton II, marking the beginning of the Olympic equestrian tradition.

Another notable event was the high jump competition, where the horse had to clear the highest possible obstacle.

In this discipline, both the horse and rider had to demonstrate incredible coordination, strength, and the ability to overcome barriers.

The inclusion of this event highlighted the skill of both horse and rider, and although such competitions already existed in society, being part of the Olympic Games gave them new legitimacy in the international sporting world.

Despite its debut in 1900, equestrian sports were not included again in the Olympic Games until 1912, at the Games held in Stockholm, Sweden, where the sport was permanently incorporated into the Olympic program.

In those Games, more organized competitions were introduced, and the disciplines that still exist today, such as show jumping, dressage, and eventing, were formalized.

These disciplines became the pillars of Olympic equestrian sports and remain part of the Olympic Games to this day.

The reason for the brief absence of equestrian sports between 1900 and 1912 was due to various factors, including the lack of a clear organizational framework and the logistics of transporting horses and equipment.

However, as the Olympic Games became more formalized and better organized, equestrian sports gained recognition and support.

Starting in 1912, the International Equestrian Federation (FEI) began overseeing Olympic equestrian competitions, establishing international standards for the events and ensuring that the competitions were fair and well-organized.

Today, equestrian events in the Olympics are a mixed sport, meaning that men and women compete together on equal terms.

This is one of the few Olympic sports where this occurs, giving it a special status within the Games.

The modern equestrian events include show jumping, dressage, and eventing, all disciplines that require great technical skill from both the rider and the horse.

Dressage, one of the most challenging disciplines, focuses on precision and control of the horse, where the animal's movements and responsiveness to the rider's subtle cues are judged.

Although this discipline was not part of the 1900 Olympic Games, it is now one of the most admired for its elegance and technical difficulty.

Show jumping, which originated from the 1900 competition, remains one of the most popular events, requiring horses to clear a series of obstacles in the shortest time possible without knocking down the bars.

# 8

**Horse racing on ice was a unique and distinctive event that was part of the 1928 Winter Olympic Games in St. Moritz.**

Although it was not an official Olympic sport in the standard program, it was included as a demonstration sport in the second Winter Olympics.

St. Moritz, located in Switzerland, is famous for its alpine climate and frozen lakes, which provided the perfect setting for this unusual discipline to be featured in the event.

Horse racing on ice, also known as skijoring, was popular in various regions of Switzerland and other Nordic countries.

In this discipline, riders guide horses that run across frozen lakes or snowy surfaces. In the most well-known variation at the time, competitors did not ride the horses directly but were instead pulled by them while gliding on skis, giving the event a unique combination of equestrian and skiing skills.

During the 1928 Games, this variation was the one presented, capturing the audience's attention with its spectacle and speed.

In St. Moritz, the races took place on a frozen lake, and the riders—or rather, skiers—were pulled by horses across an ice circuit.

This sport required great skill from both the skier and the horse

The horses had to be trained to run on icy surfaces, and the skiers needed to be able to maintain their balance and control their speed as they were pulled at high speeds over the ice.

The skijoring event at the St. Moritz Olympics was well received, and although it did not become a regular Olympic sport, it captured the public's imagination, impressing spectators with its speed and excitement.

The conditions for ice racing were dangerous, as both the horses and the skiers faced the risk of severe falls on the slippery surfaces, adding an element of danger to the event.

Although skijoring was not included in future Winter Olympic Games, it remained a popular sport in Switzerland and other alpine countries, where competitions are still held regularly, particularly in local winter events.

Notably, St. Moritz has maintained this tradition over the years, and the White Turf, an annual festival of horse racing on snow and ice held on the same lake in St. Moritz, remains one of the most anticipated events of the Swiss winter.

The White Turf includes traditional horse races as well as skijoring events, attracting spectators from around the world.

Though it has not been part of the Olympic program since then, the sport remains a distinctive element of the region and a symbol of the fusion between equestrian sports and winter sports.

One of the reasons why horse racing on ice was not included in future editions of the Winter Olympic Games was the logistical difficulty of organizing such events at different Olympic venues.

The necessary conditions, such as frozen lakes or suitable ice tracks, were not always available in every Winter Games location, making it difficult to permanently include the sport.

Additionally, the risk of injury for both the horses and the riders (or skiers) in such slippery conditions likely influenced the decision not to include this sport in future Olympic programs.

# 9

**The fastest horse breed is the Thoroughbred, known for its incredible speed and performance in horse racing.**

These horses have been carefully bred over centuries to optimize their speed, endurance, and agility, and today they dominate middle-distance races, ranging from 1,200 to 2,400 meters.

The origins of the Thoroughbred breed date back to the 17th and 18th centuries in England, when three foundational stallions were imported and crossed with local English mares.

These stallions are known as the Darley Arabian, Godolphin Arabian, and Byerley Turk, each named after their owners: Thomas Darley, Lord Godolphin, and Captain Robert Byerley.

These Arabian and Turkish horses brought speed, stamina, and agility to the genetic mix, leading to the first generation of what we now know as the Thoroughbred.

The Darley Arabian was brought to England in 1704 and is considered the most influential of the three, as approximately 95% of modern Thoroughbreds descend from him in the male line.

The Godolphin Arabian, another stallion brought to England in the early 18th century, made a significant contribution to the lineage through his offspring, especially his famous son Eclipse, who never lost a race and is the ancestor of most modern Thoroughbreds.

The Byerley Turk was originally used as a war horse, but his importance as a stallion in breeding racehorses established him as one of the pillars of the breed.

Thoroughbreds are highly versatile horses, capable of running middle distances at high speed, which requires a delicate balance between explosive speed and endurance.

Their ability to reach speeds of up to 70 km/h over short distances makes them the fastest horses in the world.

Not only are they fast, but they also have great cardiovascular endurance, which allows them to maintain a fast pace over a considerable distance—crucial for races like the Kentucky Derby or the Epsom Derby.

In terms of appearance, Thoroughbreds vary in size and height, typically measuring between 15 and 17 hands tall (one hand equals four inches or 10.16 cm).

Thoroughbred colors include chestnut, black, roan, gray, white, palomino, and various shades of dark and reddish chestnut.

Their physique is designed for speed, with slender bodies, long muscular legs, and deep chests that facilitate breathing during intense races.

One of the most interesting aspects of Thoroughbreds is that, in the breeding of this breed, artificial insemination, cloning, and embryo transfer are not allowed.

All Thoroughbreds must be conceived through natural mating to maintain the purity of the genetic line and ensure the authenticity of the breed.

This is established in the official Thoroughbred records of

The Jockey Club, which oversees the breeding and registration of these horses worldwide.

The reason behind the prohibition of artificial insemination is to preserve the integrity of the competition and ensure that Thoroughbreds remain a breed with verifiable and controlled bloodlines.

This rule guarantees that the bloodlines remain pure, without genetic alterations or manipulations that could affect the performance and quality of the breed.

Additionally, it promotes selective breeding, where only the best horses are chosen for reproduction.

In racing competitions, Thoroughbreds are the horses of choice in the world's major races, such as the Kentucky Derby in the United States, the Prix de l'Arc de Triomphe in France, and the Melbourne Cup in Australia.

They are renowned not only for their speed but also for their courage and determination on the track, enabling them to overcome obstacles and rivals with unyielding endurance.

In terms of personality, Thoroughbreds are known for their intelligence, competitiveness, and, in some cases, being temperamental due to their high energy and sensitivity.

This makes them horses that require experienced riders and patient trainers who can manage their character while making the most of their physical abilities.

# 10

**The Quarter Horse, known in English as Quarter Horse, is one of the most popular and beloved horse breeds in the world, especially in North America.**

This breed is famous for its ability to reach extremely high speeds over short distances, up to 400 meters (a quarter of a mile, hence its name).

It is considered the fastest horse breed over short distances, capable of reaching speeds of up to 88 km/h (55 mph).

Originally developed in the United State, this breed is versatile and is used in a variety of disciplines, from racing to cattle work and equestrian competitions.

The origin of the Quarter Horse dates back to colonial North America, when British settlers began crossbreeding native horses with Spanish breeds brought over by the conquistadors.

Later, settlers began importing English Thoroughbreds, which were crossed with native horses and with Arabian and Barb horses.

The goal was to produce a horse that combined the speed and agility of racehorses with the endurance and sturdiness needed for ranch work.

This crossbreeding resulted in the Quarter Horse, named for its exceptional speed over short distances of a quarter mile.

As short-distance horse racing became popular in the American colonies, Quarter Horses demonstrated their superiority over other breeds in these types of competitions.

Their ability to accelerate quickly and maintain high speeds over short distances made them favorites for this kind of race, which was often held on improvised tracks or fields.

While Thoroughbreds excel in longer distances, the Quarter Horse stood out as the fastest horse over short distances, which increased its popularity.

The Quarter Horse is not only used for racing but is also one of the most common breeds in rodeos, cutting competitions, reining events, and equestrian exhibitions where speed, agility, and responsiveness in precise movements are required.

Its agility and ability to perform quick turns and stop suddenly make it the ideal choice for cattle work.

Ranchers in the United States have relied, and continue to rely, on Quarter Horses for their ability to handle cattle quickly and effectively, which is why they are also known as "cow horses."

In terms of appearance, the Quarter Horse has a compact and muscular physique, which allows it to accelerate rapidly.

It typically stands between 14 and 16 hands tall (one hand equals 4 inches or 10.16 cm) and has a sturdy build.

Quarter Horses have a broad chest, a short back, and strong legs, which give them the perfect balance to move with agility and speed.

Their muscular appearance is one of the breed's most characteristic traits and one of the reasons they excel in disciplines that require explosive speed.

Quarter Horses can come in a wide variety of colors.

The most common colors include chestnut, sorrel, bay, black, and palomino, although the breed can also appear in rarer shades such as roan or gray.

Due to the genetic influence of other breeds, Quarter Horses can have color patterns, although solid colors are more common in the breed.

Another notable quality of this breed is its temperament.

Quarter Horses are known for being docile, intelligent, and easy to train.

This makes them excellent companions not only for experienced riders but also for beginners.

Their calm nature and willingness to work hard make them ideal for both competition activities and everyday ranch work.

They are known for their loyalty and for forming strong bonds with their owners and riders.

In the racing world, the Quarter Horse remains a dominant breed.

Quarter Horse racing, organized over short distances ranging from 220 to 870 yards, is very popular in the United States and in other countries like Mexico and Brazil.

Although they don't have the same duration or fame as

Thoroughbred races, Quarter Horse races attract a large number of fans due to the spectacular nature of the competitions, which are fast, exciting, and action-packed.

Quarter Horses can surpass the speed of Thoroughbreds over these short distances, adding a level of intensity to the races.

In terms of breeding, the Quarter Horse breed is regulated and registered by the American Quarter Horse Association (AQHA), founded in 1940.

This organization is responsible for maintaining the breed's standards, promoting its growth, and ensuring that the distinctive characteristics of the Quarter Horse are preserved over time.

The AQHA is one of the largest horse registries in the world, and its efforts have helped spread the popularity of the Quarter Horse beyond North America.

In addition to their use in rodeos and racing, Quarter Horses are commonly used for recreational riding due to their reliability and versatility.

Thanks to their calm temperament and ease of adaptation to various situations, they are ideal for leisurely rides, trail excursions, and family equestrian activities.

This versatility has contributed to making them one of the most popular and beloved horse breeds worldwide.

# 11

**The Akhal Teke is one of the world's oldest and most exotic horse breeds, originating from the region of Turkmenistan in Central Asia.**

This horse is famous for its endurance, speed, and physical beauty, with a distinctive metallic coat that sets it apart from other breeds.

The Akhal Teke is known for its ability to withstand extreme climatic conditions, which allowed it to survive and thrive in the harsh desert lands of Central Asia.

These horses have a rich and mystical history, linking them to ancient nomadic peoples and their use in war, hunting, and trade routes.

The breed's name comes from the Teke tribe, one of the Turkmen nomadic tribes that inhabited the Akhal oasis region, along the Karakum Desert.

The Teke tribe developed these horses over thousands of years, selecting the most resilient and fastest specimens.

For centuries, Akhal Teke horses were considered treasures of the Turkmen tribes, valued not only for their use in battle but also as symbols of status and wealth.

The Akhal Teke is an extremely hardy breed, renowned for its ability to endure long journeys with little food and water, a trait that was vital for the nomadic desert peoples.

These horses were bred in very harsh conditions, which allowed them to develop exceptional physical endurance and remarkable agility.

On many occasions, Akhal Teke horses were kept covered and protected from the extreme desert elements to preserve their energy and keep their musculature in optimal condition.

One of the most striking features of the Akhal Teke is its shiny, metallic coat, which gives it a unique and spectacular appearance.

This characteristic is especially visible in lighter colors such as golden, palomino, and bay, though it can also be found in darker tones like black and chestnut.

The metallic shine of the Akhal Teke's coat is due to the structure of its hair, which reflects light in a special way, giving it an almost iridescent appearance.

This trait has earned the Akhal Teke the nickname "the golden horse."

In terms of physique, the Akhal Teke is known for having a slender and elegant, yet very muscular body. Horses of this breed are tall, with an average height of 15 to 16 hands (about 152 to 162 cm).

They have a long, arched neck, a fine, dry head, large, expressive eyes, and long ears.

Their limbs are long and thin but extremely strong, giving them great agility and maneuverability.

This combination of strength and elegance allows them to excel in equestrian sports as well as more demanding activities like racing and endurance riding.

The character of the Akhal Teke is one of its most admired traits. They are extremely loyal horses and form a close bond with their owners.

It is said that Akhal Teke horses are sensitive and respond

well to kind and respectful treatment, but they also require an experienced rider, as they have an independent nature and can sometimes be difficult to manage if not handled properly.

This combination of sensitivity and independence makes them unique horses, valued both for their beauty and their strong personality.

In ancient times, the Akhal Teke was prized for its speed and endurance, qualities that made it the ideal horse for long expeditions across the desert and for military campaigns.

They are considered ancestors of several modern horse breeds, including Thoroughbreds and Arabians.

For centuries, these horses were used by Turkmen warriors for swift attacks and retreats in battle, contributing to their reputation as war horses.

They were also known for participating in long-distance races, where their endurance allowed them to outlast other breeds over difficult terrain and in extreme conditions.

Throughout history, the Akhal Teke has been a horse of royalty and legend.

It is said that the Persian emperor Darius I of ancient Persia rode horses similar to the Akhal Teke in his campaigns.

These horses were also believed to have been offered as gifts to emperors and leaders in ancient China, solidifying their status as a prestigious and revered breed.

In more modern times, Akhal Tekes have proven their worth in endurance competitions.

One of the most famous events that demonstrated the endurance of this breed was an epic race that took place in 1935, when a group of Turkmen riders and their Akhal Teke horses completed a 4,300-kilometer journey from Ashgabat (Turkmenistan) to Moscow in 84 days, crossing the Karakum Desert with barely any water supply.

This event was a testament to the incredible endurance of the Akhal Teke, confirming its reputation as the most resilient long-distance horse breed.

In modern equestrian sports, the Akhal Teke has excelled in disciplines such as dressage and endurance.

Their lightweight body and agility make them well-suited for sports that require precise and elegant movements.

Although they are not as common in jumping competitions or short-distance races, their endurance and ability to cover long distances have made them highly valued in endurance trials.

Today, the Akhal Teke remains a symbol of national pride in Turkmenistan.

The Turkmen government protects and promotes the breeding of this horse, and the Akhal Teke is even the national emblem of the country.

There are statues and monuments dedicated to these horses, and each year festivals and events are held to honor this unique breed.

# 12

**The Arabian horse is one of the world's oldest and most recognized horse breeds, famous for its endurance, elegance, and character.**

Originating from West Asia, the Arabian horse was developed by the Bedouins, who specifically bred it to cover long distances across the desert.

These horses were essential for the survival of the nomadic peoples, allowing them to travel great distances quickly, escape enemies, and conduct raids.

Arabians were selected for their endurance and speed over difficult terrain, making them the preferred breed for long journeys.

The Arabian horse has a unique physical structure that gives it a significant advantage in terms of endurance and long-distance travel.

Unlike other breeds, the Arabian has a high number of Type I muscle fibers, which are slow-twitch fibers.

These fibers enable the horse's muscles to work for long periods without tiring, making them ideal for endurance competitions and the long journeys that characterized Bedouin life in the desert.

Additionally, Arabian horses have less muscle mass than other breeds, such as the Quarter Horse, allowing them to move more efficiently and maintain a steady pace over long distances

The Arabian horse is also known for its skeletal structure.

It has a compact body, with a short, straight back, a deep chest that allows for great lung capacity and, therefore, excellent oxygenation during exercise.

Its profile is easily recognizable, with a small, refined head, large expressive eyes, small ears, and an arched neck.

Additionally, Arabians have a high tail carriage and an elegant posture, giving them a majestic appearance when in motion.

The endurance of the Arabian horse was crucial for long journeys across the desert, where extreme temperatures and limited water supply required horses that could keep moving with little food or hydration.

This ability to withstand harsh conditions, along with their docile and loyal nature, made them indispensable companions for nomadic peoples.

The Bedouins even allowed their horses to sleep in their tents, fostering a strong bond between rider and animal.

Over the centuries, the Arabian horse spread beyond its homeland, influencing many other horse breeds around the world.

Thoroughbreds, Andalusians, and many other breeds carry Arabian genes in their lineage, demonstrating the influence and versatility of this breed.

The speed and agility of Arabian horses made them an important genetic foundation for improving other breeds, especially in racing and endurance competitions.

In 1725, the first Arabian horses were brought to North America.

However, it wasn't until after the American Civil War that the breeding of Arabians as a pure breed began to gain importance.

During this period, Arabian horses were registered with the Jockey Club in a separate subsection from Thoroughbreds.

This allowed the breed to remain distinct, although at that time, there was no formal registry dedicated exclusively to Arabians in America.

Finally, in 1908, the Arabian Horse Registry of America was formed, establishing guidelines for the breeding and preservation of the breed on the continent.

Today, the Arabian horse is best known for its use in endurance racing.

Endurance racing is an equestrian sport where horses and riders cover long distances (typically between 40 and 160 kilometers) over challenging terrain, and Arabians have proven to be unmatched in this discipline.

Their ability to maintain a steady pace for long hours, their natural endurance, and their ability to recover quickly make the Arabian horse the dominant breed in this category.

Although endurance racing is the primary use for the Arabian horse today, this breed also competes in traditional racetrack events, though they do not possess the same explosive speed as Thoroughbreds.

In many countries, especially in the Middle East, where the breed is revered, Arabian horse racing is an important part of equestrian sport.

These races are governed by the International Federation of Arabian Horse Racing Authorities (IFAHR), which regulates competitions and promotes the breeding of Arabian horses worldwide.

Arabian horses not only excel in sports competitions but are also highly valued for their temperament.

They are known for being intelligent, docile, and loyal, making them ideal horses for a variety of disciplines, including dressage, recreational riding, and equestrian shows.

Their temperament makes them suitable for riders of all levels, from beginners to experts.

Another distinguishing aspect of the Arabian horse is its longevity and overall health.

Arabians tend to live longer than other horse breeds and are known for their resistance to disease and their ability to maintain vitality into old age.

This makes them particularly valuable as working horses and for recreational activities.

As for the breed's colors, Arabian horses can exhibit a variety of coat colors, including bay, chestnut, gray, and black.

However, gray is one of the most characteristic and popular colors in the breed, often associated with the classic image of Arabian horses in popular culture.

# 13

**It is likely that horses do not have a concept of "being in a race" in the way humans understand it—meaning a competition with the goal of surpassing others and being the first to reach the finish line.**

Running, or galloping, is a natural behavior for horses, and in the wild, they do so instinctively, either to escape predators or simply as part of their social behavior within a group.

Running in groups is something horses do voluntarily when given the opportunity, and in nature, they do it to synchronize with other herd members, which provides them with a greater sense of security.

Arriving first or separating from the group, on the other hand, could be disadvantageous in the wild, as straying from the group exposes a horse to a greater risk of predation.

In a professional horse race, although horses do not understand that they are in a "competition" in the human sense, they learn through training and experience what is expected of them during a race.

Horses are highly trainable and responsive animals, and they can learn to associate the dynamics of a race (the increase in speed, cues from the jockey, the excitement in the environment) with a certain pattern of behavior.

In this way, although they do not have a conscious desire to "win," horses can be trained to respond to the jockey's signals and maintain competitive behavior during the race.

Trainers and jockeys, in fact, take advantage of horses' natural tendencies to synchronize with other horses but train them to ignore this instinctive tendency at certain moments.

Horses have different racing styles and individual preferences, which trainers learn to identify to maximize the horse's performance.

For example, some horses prefer to run at the front of the group from the start; these are called front-runners.

Others, on the contrary, feel more comfortable running in a group, benefiting from the security and collective pace until they near the end of the race; these are known as come-from-behind runners.

What is clear is that horses learn to recognize what happens during a race.

Although they do not understand the concept of "competition," they do learn, through experience and training, that the dynamics of a race involve certain behavior patterns: running fast, responding to the jockey's cues, and adjusting to what is happening around them.

Jockeys play a crucial role in guiding the horse throughout the race, adjusting speed and making strategic decisions based on the individual characteristics of the animal and the conditions of the race.

This learning and training largely explain a horse's performance in a race.

In other words, a horse's success in a race does not depend on an innate desire to win, but rather on a combination of factors such as its natural ability, physical fitness, the training it has received, and the jockey's ability to make strategic decisions during the race.

Additionally, the jockey's ability to understand the horse's preferences is crucial.

Every horse has a personality and running style that can influence its performance on the track.

Some horses may enjoy being at the front, feeling comfortable with the pressure of leading the race, while others prefer to stay behind the group until the end approaches, when they feel more confident to accelerate and attempt to win.

# 14

**In terms of physical performance, adult horses have impressive athletic abilities.**

At a gallop, an average horse can reach a speed of around 44 km/h (27 mph), which is already a considerable feat.

The gallop is the fastest gait of a horse, a four-beat stride in which the hooves strike the ground in a coordinated pattern, allowing for rapid coverage of ground.

This ability has served them throughout history, both in the wild and in human activities such as transportation, warfare, farming, and, of course, racing.

However, some horses have far exceeded this average speed, achieving truly remarkable feats.

One of the most notable examples is the fastest horse on record, which reached a speed of 88 km/h (55 mph).

This record was achieved over short distances, typically under controlled conditions and with horses specifically trained for sprinting.

Thoroughbreds are the most famous for breaking speed records, especially in short-distance races where they can unleash their maximum speed before becoming fatigued.

This level of speed places horses among the fastest animals on the planet.

Although they are not as fast as some felines, like the cheetah, their ability to maintain a fast pace over longer distances is impressive.

In addition to their speed at a gallop, horses also excel in endurance, able to cover long distances at moderate speeds without tiring, which has made them ideal companions for long journeys throughout history.

The physique of a horse is perfectly adapted for running.

They have powerful, long muscles in their legs, allowing them to take long strides and generate a great deal of power with each hoof strike.

Additionally, they possess a highly efficient cardiovascular system, which enables them to keep their heart rate and respiratory system stable even when running at high speeds.

Their large lungs and strong heart ensure they can oxygenate their muscles during long races, which is crucial for both speed races and endurance events.

In terms of biomechanics, horses are designed to maximize the efficiency of the gallop.

The coordination of their limbs and the way their spine flexes during galloping allow them to fully extend their front and hind legs, increasing the length of each stride.

A horse's ability to adjust the frequency and length of its stride depending on the terrain and conditions also contributes to its speed and overall performance.

The fastest horse breeds, such as Thoroughbreds, have been selected and bred over centuries to enhance their speed and endurance abilities.

Thoroughbreds are known for their capacity to run at high speeds over short to medium distances.

On the other hand, breeds like Arabian horses are known for their ability to maintain a moderately fast pace over long distances, making them stand out in endurance races.

The record of 88 km/h is a testament to the extreme athletic ability some horses can achieve, but it's important to note that this speed can only be sustained for very short periods, typically over distances of less than 400 meters.

This type of speed is most common in short-distance races, where an explosive burst of speed is crucial for success.

Horses used in sprint races are specifically trained to develop that explosiveness in their muscles, with training routines focused on maximizing strength and speed over short stretches.

In addition to their natural speed, a horse's performance is also heavily influenced by external factors such as terrain, weather conditions, and the jockey's weight.

The type of track they run on, whether dirt, turf, or sand, can affect their maximum speed and the way they move.

Horses tend to be faster on well-maintained tracks, where the surface is soft but not too slippery.

Weather conditions, such as humidity and temperature, can also influence performance, as extreme heat or rain can affect the horse's comfort and health.

Training and diet play a fundamental role in developing a horse's speed.

Trainers adjust exercise programs, ensuring that horses develop not only the right musculature but also the endurance needed for racing.

Racehorses often have special diets rich in proteins, vitamins, and minerals to ensure their muscles can recover quickly after physical exertion.

Another key factor in a horse's speed is the jockey.

An experienced jockey knows how to position themselves to minimize wind resistance and how to guide the horse in a way that maximizes speed without wasting too much energy at the wrong moments.

Moreover, the jockey's ability to synchronize with the horse and handle pressure during the race can make the difference between winning and losing, as a jockey can help the horse maintain a steady pace or give it the necessary push in the final moments of the race.

# 15

**The most expensive horses
in the history of horse racing.**

**1. Fusaichi Pegasus:** This horse is considered the most expensive horse in history, sold for a record sum of $70 million in the year 2000. Fusaichi Pegasus won the Kentucky Derby in 2000 and was acquired by the breeding operation Coolmore Stud with the hope that he would become an extremely valuable stallion. Although he didn't achieve the expected success in breeding, he remains the most expensive horse ever sold.

**2. Shareef Dancer:** In 1983, Shareef Dancer was sold for $40 million. This Thoroughbred, born in 1980 and owned by the Emir of Dubai, won several important races in Europe and was purchased for his breeding potential. Although his career as a stallion was moderately successful, his sale was one of the most notable moments in horse auction history.

**3. The Green Monkey:** One of the most famous horses for its high price and disappointing performance. The Green Monkey was sold for $16 million at auction in 2006. Despite his impressive breeding credentials, the horse never won a race in his short career. This example shows that in horse racing, genetic promise does not always translate to success on the track.

**4. Seattle Dancer:** This horse set a world auction record in 1985 when he was sold for $13.1 million. Seattle Dancer had an impressive pedigree, being the son of the legendary Nijinsky II. Although he was not a great runner, he had moderate success as a stallion, producing some competitive offspring.

**5. Meydan City:** Sold for $11.7 million in 2006, Meydan City was acquired by Sheikh Mohammed bin Rashid Al Maktoum for his Godolphin operation. Despite a strong pedigree, Meydan City did not live up to expectations on the track, once again highlighting that a high purchase price doesn't always translate to racing success.

**6. Palloubet d'Halong:** Although not specifically a racehorse, this show jumping horse was sold for $15 million. He is one of the most expensive horses in the world due to his success in equestrian jumping competitions, demonstrating that in the broader world of equestrian sports, exceptional horses can command extraordinarily high prices.

**7. Snaafi Dancer:** Sold for $10.2 million in 1983, Snaafi Dancer was acquired by Sheikh Mohammed of Dubai, associated with Alydar. However, he turned out to be a failure both in racing and breeding, as he never competed and had fertility issues, making him one of the most disappointing investments in sports history.

**8. Jalil:** Acquired by Sheikh Mohammed bin Rashid Al Maktoum for $9.7 million in 2005. Although Jalil wasn't exceptional on the track, he did win some important races and was retired to stand as a stallion in Dubai.

**9. Plavius:** Sold for $9.2 million at auction in 2006, Plavius was also purchased by Godolphin Racing. Despite his high price tag, he failed to stand out on the racetrack, and his racing career was relatively unremarkable.

**10. Moorlands Totilas:** Though not a racehorse, Totilas, known for his excellence in dressage, was sold for $9.5 million.

This horse is an example of how equestrian sport horses, beyond racing, can reach extremely high prices due to their achievements in competitions.

**11. Marju:** Sold for $9.2 million in 1989, Marju was acquired for his impressive lineage and breeding potential. Although he had a relatively successful racing career, highlighted by a win in the Irish Derby, his true value lay in his ability to pass on strong genes to his offspring.

**12. Makybe Diva:** Although not sold for a record sum, Makybe Diva was valued at $8.5 million after becoming a racing legend as the only mare to win the Melbourne Cup three times (2003, 2004, and 2005). Her success on the track significantly increased her value as a broodmare.

**13. Justify:** Sold for $60 million as a stallion, Justify is one of the most valuable horses in the world after winning the Triple Crown in 2018. Although not sold at a public auction, his stud agreement makes him one of the most expensive horses in recent history.

**14. Frankel:** Although never sold at auction, Frankel is considered one of the most valuable horses in history due to his undefeated record in 14 races, including multiple Group 1 wins. His value as a stallion is estimated at over $100 million, thanks to his extraordinary genetics and status as one of the greatest racehorses of all time. Each of his stud services costs hundreds of thousands of dollars, making him one of the most sought-after and valuable stallions in the industry.

# 16

**Cheating and fixing in horse racing.**

**1. Kieren Fallon:** One of the most notorious cases in horse racing involved British jockey Kieren Fallon, a six-time champion in the UK. In 2006, Fallon was accused of conspiring to fix races to benefit bettors, in what became known as the "race-fixing scandal." It was suspected that Fallon, along with other jockeys and trainers, manipulated races by preventing favored horses from winning, benefiting those who bet against them. Although he was arrested and taken to trial, he was acquitted due to a lack of conclusive evidence. Nevertheless, this case damaged his reputation and cast a shadow over his career.

**2. Patrick Biancone**: In 2007, French trainer Patrick Biancone was suspended for a year after snake venom and other prohibited substances were found in his stable in the United States. These substances were intended to numb the pain of horses, allowing them to race without feeling physical discomfort. This case was particularly shocking due to the dangerous nature of the substances used. Biancone, who had achieved success training high-level horses, was severely punished, and the incident highlighted the risks and cheating involved in manipulating horses to gain an advantage in races.

**3. Lester Piggott:** While not accused of race-fixing, Lester Piggott, one of the most successful and legendary jockeys of all time with nine Epsom Derby victories, was convicted of tax fraud in 1987. Piggott hid his earnings to avoid paying taxes, leading to a prison sentence. Although it didn't directly affect his performances on the track, this scandal damaged Lester Piggott's reputation and resulted in the loss of his jockey title. He was temporarily suspended, and while his return to the sport after prison was notable, the scandal remains a black mark on his career.

**4. Jorge Navarro:** In 2018, trainer Jorge Navarro was accused of using illegal drugs on his horses to enhance their performance. Investigations revealed that Navarro used substances that improved the stamina and performance of his horses, giving him an unfair advantage over his competitors. Navarro was suspended and became a symbol of doping scandals in horse racing. This case was part of a larger investigation involving multiple trainers and veterinarians in the United States, shedding light on dishonest practices in the industry.

**5. The Green Monkey:** A horse sold for $16 million was also involved in controversy. Although not directly related to cheating on the track, it was a notable case because the horse never lived up to the high expectations associated with its enormous price. Suspicions arose that his success had been deliberately overhyped to inflate his auction price. While there was no proof of foul play, the case highlights how manipulating a horse's reputation can be a form of fraud.

**6. Snaafi Dancer:** The horse Snaafi Dancer, purchased for over $10 million in the 1980s, became a scandal in the racing world. He never raced due to fertility issues, leading to suspicions of fraud surrounding his purchase. Snaafi Dancer's inability to race or breed raised concerns about the transparency of transactions at horse auctions and sparked questions about the manipulation of genetic information to artificially inflate the value of certain horses.

**7. Godolphin Racing Doping Scandal:** In 2013, the renowned Godolphin Racing stable was hit by a major doping scandal when its trainer, Mahmood Al Zarooni, was suspended for eight years after it was discovered that he had administered anabolic steroids to 11 horses. This scandal affected one of the world's most successful and prestigious stables, run by Sheikh Mohammed bin Rashid Al Maktoum. Al Zarooni was responsible for some of the most prominent horses, and the doping scandal severely damaged the stable's reputation.

**8. Ryan Moore:** While there have been no formal accusations of race-fixing, British jockey Ryan Moore, one of the most successful in the world, has been the subject of past criticism for alleged tactical performances in races where he did not behave as expected. However, in most cases, there has been no conclusive evidence, and Moore remains one of the most respected jockeys on the circuit.

**9. Billy Walters Horse Racing Scandal:** More linked to betting than direct cheating, gambler Billy Walters was one of the largest investors in horse racing in the United States and was involved in several race-fixing and illegal betting scandals in the 1980s and 1990s. Walters used insider information to influence race outcomes, working in collusion with jockeys and trainers to manipulate bets in his favor.

**10. Willie Mullins:** The famous Irish trainer Willie Mullins, although not accused of race-fixing, was at the center of rumors of cheating when several of his horses were accused of unclear performances on the National Hunt circuit. These rumors, however, never resulted in formal accusations, and Mullins continues to be one of the most successful trainers in Europe.

# 17

**The Kentucky Derby is one of the most prestigious and oldest horse races in the world, held annually at Churchill Downs racetrack in Louisville, Kentucky.**

Since its founding in 1875 by Meriwether Lewis Clark Jr., the Derby has become an iconic event in the sport of horse racing, known not only for the competition on the track but also for the tradition, fashion, and culture that surround it.

Meriwether Lewis Clark Jr., grandson of the famous explorer William Clark, was inspired to create the Derby after visiting Europe, where he attended horse races, particularly the Epsom Derby in England.

Upon returning to the United States, he decided to build a racetrack in Louisville, naming it Churchill Downs in honor of his family, who owned the land.

The first Kentucky Derby was held on May 17, 1875, with an original distance of 1 ½ miles (2,400 meters), similar to the Epsom Derby.

In 1896, the distance was shortened to 1 ¼ miles (2,000 meters), which remains the current length of the race.

The Kentucky Derby is the first race of the prestigious Triple Crown of American horse racing, followed by the Preakness Stakes and the Belmont Stakes.

Only three-year-old Thoroughbreds are eligible to

compete in the Derby, making each edition a unique event.

The race takes place on the first Saturday of May and attracts a crowd of more than 150,000 spectators each year, making it one of the most attended sporting events in the United States.

One of the most notable features of the Kentucky Derby is the fashion that surrounds it.

Attendees typically wear elegant outfits and adorn their heads with exotic and eye-catching hats.

These hats have become an iconic tradition of the event, with designs ranging from the most sophisticated to the most extravagant and quirky.

This trend originated as a way to emulate British high society, but over time it has evolved into a fundamental part of the Derby experience.

Another important cultural aspect of the Derby is the Mint Julep, the official drink of the event.

This cocktail is made with bourbon, mint, sugar, and water, and is traditionally served in silver or pewter cups.

Attendees enjoy thousands of Mint Juleps each year during Derby weekend, and the drink has become as iconic as the race itself.

The Derby is also famous for its unofficial anthem, "My Old Kentucky Home," which is sung before the race begins.

This moment evokes a sense of tradition and nostalgia among the spectators and is part of the ritual that precedes the competition.

As for the race itself, the Kentucky Derby is known as "the most exciting two minutes in sports," as the race typically lasts around two minutes.

Over the years, there have been legendary horses that have made history on this track, including Triple Crown winners like Secretariat, American Pharoah, and Justify.

The speed record for the Derby was set by Secretariat in 1973, when he completed the race in 1:59.40 minutes, a time that remains unbeaten.

The Kentucky Derby has also been the setting for historic moments in horse racing and sports.

One of the most memorable occurred in 1915, when Regret became the first filly to win the Derby.

Another historic moment happened in 2009, when Mine That Bird, with 50-1 odds, pulled off one of the greatest upsets in Derby history by winning the race after a spectacular charge from the back of the pack.

Beyond the track, the Kentucky Derby has had a significant impact on the economy and culture of Louisville.

The event draws visitors from around the world, generating millions of dollars in revenue for the city.

In addition to the main race, Derby week includes multiple social events and festivals, such as the Kentucky Derby Festival, which features parades, exhibits, and community activities.

The betting culture also plays a major role in the Kentucky Derby.

It is one of the largest betting events in the United States, with spectators both at the racetrack and across the country wagering millions of dollars on the horses.

Bets are placed on both the favorites and the underdogs, which adds to the excitement of the race.

# 18

**Secretariat is one of the most legendary racehorses of all time and is known for holding the record for the fastest race in the Kentucky Derby, with a time of 1 minute and 59.4 seconds.**

This record was set on May 5, 1973, during the 99th edition of the Derby, and remains unbeaten to this day.

Secretariat, an American Thoroughbred, is celebrated not only for his speed but also for his imposing physique and absolute dominance on the track, particularly in the three races that make up the Triple Crown.

Nicknamed "Big Red" due to his striking chestnut coat, Secretariat was trained by Lucien Laurin and ridden by jockey Ron Turcotte.

His race in the 1973 Kentucky Derby was a historic moment, not only because of his victory but also for the manner in which he achieved it.

In that race, Secretariat not only broke the overall record but also did something unheard of: each quarter-mile he ran was faster than the previous one.

This is a testament to his ability to continuously accelerate throughout the race, setting him apart from most horses, which typically slow down in the final stretch.

After his triumph in the Derby, Secretariat continued on his path to the Triple Crown, winning the Preakness Stakes and the Belmont Stakes, becoming the first horse in 25 years to win all three races.

His performance in the Belmont Stakes was perhaps even more impressive than in the Kentucky Derby.

Secretariat not only won the race, but did so by an astounding margin of 31 lengths, which remains the largest victory margin in Triple Crown history.

Additionally, he completed the race in 2 minutes and 24 seconds, setting yet another record that also remains unbeaten.

Secretariat's record in the Kentucky Derby stands out not only for the time itself, but for the way he controlled the race.

At the start, he began at the back of the pack, an unusual tactic for a favored horse, but as the race progressed, he steadily and strategically gained ground, accelerating towards the finish.

This style of racing made his victory seem inevitable, despite starting behind other competitors.

Throughout his racing career, Secretariat won 16 of his 21 races, including titles such as Horse of the Year in 1972 and 1973, and he was inducted into the Jockey Club Hall of Fame in 1974.

In addition to his success on the track, Secretariat made an impact as a stallion in the horse racing industry.

Although his success as a sire was not as dominant as his racing career, he produced several notable offspring that continued his legacy.

Secretariat is considered one of the most complete horses in the history of the sport, known for his speed, endurance, and winning mentality.

His physique was also impressive: he stood around 1.68 meters tall (about 16.2 hands) and weighed approximately 500 kilograms (around 1,100 pounds).

Studies conducted after his death revealed that his heart was twice the size of an average horse's heart, which may have given him an advantage in terms of endurance and oxygenation during races.

Secretariat's impact on the sport goes beyond his records.

He became a cultural icon in the United States, and his story has been the subject of books, documentaries, and the successful Disney movie "Secretariat" in 2010, which tells the story of his incredible journey.

His legacy in the world of horse racing is so influential that even decades after his last race, he is still considered the standard by which all other horses are measured.

In addition to his records in the Kentucky Derby and Belmont Stakes, Secretariat is also the only horse to win the Triple Crown with record times in all three races.

His time in the Preakness Stakes was initially not recognized as an official record due to a timer malfunction, but subsequent reviews confirmed that his race time also set a new standard.

# 19

**Impressive records achieved by racehorses.**

**1. Man o' War:** Considered one of the greatest racehorses of all time, Man o' War won 20 of 21 races between 1919 and 1920. Although he didn't race in the Kentucky Derby, Man o' War was famous for his speed and dominance on the track. He set several speed records in races such as the Belmont Stakes, where he won by 20 lengths. One of his most impressive records was in the 1920 Lawrence Realization Stakes, where he won by 100 lengths, a record that is still talked about in the racing world today.

**2. American Pharoah:** In 2015, American Pharoah became the first horse to win the Triple Crown (Kentucky Derby, Preakness Stakes, and Belmont Stakes) since 1978, and then made history by winning the Breeders' Cup Classic in the same year, achieving what is known as the "Grand Slam" of horse racing. In the Belmont Stakes, he won by 5 ½ lengths and posted an impressive time of 2 minutes and 26.65 seconds. His victory in the Breeders' Cup Classic was also remarkable, completing the race in 2 minutes and 0.07 seconds, solidifying his status as one of the greatest horses in history.

**3. Citation:** Champion in 1948, Citation was the first horse to earn over $1 million in prize money during his career. He was also the eighth horse to win the Triple Crown and achieved an impressive record by winning 16 consecutive races. His consistency and dominance placed him among the greatest racehorses, being one of the most successful of his era.

**4. Seabiscuit:** Although he never won the Triple Crown, his record and popularity were immense during the 1930s.

Seabiscuit set several track records, particularly at Santa Anita and other tracks in California. He became famous for his victory over champion War Admiral in the legendary Match Race of 1938, where he defeated the then-favorite War Admiral in an exciting head-to-head battle.

**5. Zenyatta:** One of the most legendary mares in the history of horse racing, Zenyatta won 19 of 20 races and became the first mare to win the Breeders' Cup Classic in 2009, defeating fierce competition in an epic race. Her streak of consecutive victories, including multiple Breeders' Cup races, made her one of the most successful and respected mares in the sport.

**6. Frankel:** Trained by Sir Henry Cecil in the UK, he is considered one of the greatest horses in British racing history. Frankel finished his career undefeated, winning 14 out of 14 races. His final race in the Champion Stakes in 2012 was one of the most thrilling moments in the sport, and he was recognized for his speed and power on the track. In 2011, Frankel set an impressive record in the Queen Elizabeth II Stakes, delivering a performance that cemented his status as one of the most dominant horses in Europe.

**7. Winx:** The Australian mare Winx made history by winning 33 consecutive races, including four Cox Plates, one of Australia's most prestigious races. This streak of consecutive victories, along with her impressive ability to dominate her rivals, made her a legend in the equestrian world, both in Australia and globally. Her consistency and ability to win at Australia's most important tracks made her one of the most successful mares of all time.

**8. Cigar:** Known for winning 16 consecutive races between 1994 and 1996, including the Breeders' Cup Classic in 1995.

He was named Horse of the Year twice, and at the time of his retirement, Cigar had earned over $10 million in prize money, setting a record at that time. His dominance on U.S. tracks made him one of the most recognized horses of the 1990s.

**9. Ruffian:** The mare Ruffian is remembered as one of the fastest and most talented fillies in racing history. She won 10 of 11 races, and in each of her victories, she equaled or broke track records. Tragically, Ruffian suffered a fatal injury in a Match Race against Foolish Pleasure in 1975, which led to her death shortly after. Despite her short career, she is still remembered as one of the fastest and most dominant fillies.

**10. Phar Lap:** One of the most famous horses from Australia and New Zealand, Phar Lap won 37 of 51 races and was known for dominating the tracks in the early 1930s. He won the Melbourne Cup in 1930 and became a symbol of inspiration for millions during the Great Depression. Although he died under mysterious circumstances in 1932, his legacy endures in the racing world.

**11. Northern Dancer:** One of the most important horses in Thoroughbred breeding history. He won the Kentucky Derby in 1964 with a time of 2:00 minutes, which was the third-fastest time in history at that point. What truly distinguishes Northern Dancer is his legacy as a stallion. He was the sire or grandsire of a long list of champion racehorses worldwide, and many of his descendants have won elite races. His influence in breeding remains dominant today, and his bloodline is considered one of the most valuable in the world of horse racing.

**12. Affirmed:** He is remembered for winning the Triple Crown in 1978, defeating his rival Alydar in each of the three races (Kentucky Derby, Preakness Stakes, and

Belmont Stakes). The rivalry between Affirmed and Alydar is one of the most legendary in the history of the sport, with Alydar finishing second in all three Triple Crown races. Affirmed won a total of 22 out of 29 races and was named Horse of the Year twice. He was also the last horse to win the Triple Crown until the feat was repeated 37 years later by American Pharoah in 2015.

**13. Alydar:** He is considered one of the greatest horses to never win the Triple Crown. Although he finished second to Affirmed in all three Triple Crown races in 1978, Alydar is remembered for his incredible consistency and talent. Over his career, he won 14 out of 26 races and went on to become a highly successful stallion. His influence in Thoroughbred breeding has been significant, with many of his descendants becoming champions on the track.

**14. Ghostzapper:** He was one of the fastest horses of his generation. Ghostzapper won the Breeders' Cup Classic in 2004 with a time of 1:59.02, one of the fastest times in the history of the race. He won 9 out of 11 races during his career, and his speed and versatility made him a champion at distances ranging from 7 furlongs to 1¼ miles. He was named Horse of the Year in 2004 and is considered one of the fastest horses in the history of American racing.

**15. Spectacular Bid:** He was one of the most dominant horses of the late 1970s and early 1980s. Spectacular Bid won the Kentucky Derby and the Preakness Stakes in 1979, but his bid for the Triple Crown was thwarted when he finished third in the Belmont Stakes due to a foot injury. Over his career, he won 26 out of 30 races, including multiple track records. In 1980, he set a track record at Santa Anita with a time of 1:57.8 for 1¼ miles, which remains one of the fastest times ever recorded for that distance.

**16. Dr. Fager:** A standout American racehorse of the 1960s, Dr. Fager was known for his incredible speed and versatility across different distances. In 1968, Dr. Fager set a world record for one mile with a time of 1:32.20, a record that stood for many years. He won 18 of 22 races during his career and was named Horse of the Year in 1968. What makes Dr. Fager unique is that he won titles in multiple categories, including Sprinter of the Year, Champion Miler, and Champion Handicap Horse.

**17. Sunday Silence:** One of the best racehorses of the late 1980s, Sunday Silence won the Japanese Triple Crown and the Kentucky Derby and Preakness Stakes in 1989. Although he lost the Belmont Stakes, missing the U.S. Triple Crown, he won the Breeders' Cup Classic that same year, cementing his status as one of the most successful horses of his time. What truly made Sunday Silence special was his success as a sire, especially in Japan, where he became one of the most influential stallions of all time.

**18. Kelso:** A legendary horse, Kelso won the Horse of the Year title for five consecutive years, from 1960 to 1964, a record that still stands. Although he never won the Triple Crown, his consistency over a long career made him one of the most successful horses of all time. Kelso won 39 out of 63 races and was known for excelling in long-distance races, winning events up to 2 miles.

**19. Arrogate:** He is remembered for his dominant performances in some of the world's most prestigious races. In 2016, Arrogate won the Breeders' Cup Classic and set a new record in the Travers Stakes with a time of 1:59.36 for 1¼ miles, surpassing Secretariat's record in the same race. In 2017, Arrogate won the Pegasus World Cup and the Dubai World Cup, making him the most financially successful horse at the time, with earnings of over $17 million.

# 20

**Alonzo "Lonnie" Clayton holds the record as the youngest jockey to win the Kentucky Derby, achieving this incredible feat at the age of 15 in 1892.**

Lonnie Clayton became a historic figure in the world of horse racing, not only for his youth but also for his natural talent and success in a sport that, at the time, was dominated by African American jockeys.

Clayton was born in 1876 in Kansas City, Missouri, and developed an interest in horse racing at an early age, following in the footsteps of his older brother, Albertus Clayton, who was also a jockey.

Lonnie demonstrated an innate ability to ride horses from a young age and quickly made a name for himself on the racing circuit.

By the age of 14, he was already considered one of the most promising jockeys in the country, and just a year later, at 15, he achieved his greatest triumph: winning the Kentucky Derby.

The 1892 Kentucky Derby was the 18th edition of the race, and Clayton rode Azra, trained by John H. Morris.

Despite his youth, Clayton displayed remarkable maturity and skill on the track.

He guided Azra to victory in a close race, defeating much more experienced jockeys.

This victory catapulted him to fame and cemented his status as one of the top stars in horse racing at that time.

What is remarkable about Clayton's story is that he was part of a distinguished group of African American jockeys who dominated horse racing in the late 19th century.

In the early decades of the Kentucky Derby, many of the best jockeys were African American, and several of them won the prestigious race.

In fact, between 1875 and 1902, 15 of the first 28 Kentucky Derby winners were ridden by African American jockeys.

Lonnie Clayton was part of this legacy and played a crucial role in the history of horse racing.

Despite his early success, Clayton's career began to decline after the 1890s, as racial segregation and structural racism increasingly impacted the world of horse racing.

African American jockeys began to be marginalized, and like many of his contemporaries, Clayton found it increasingly difficult to secure rides in major events.

However, he continued to race for several years after his Derby victory.

Lonnie Clayton's career is remembered not only for his Kentucky Derby win at such a young age, but also as a reflection of the changing history of the sport and the pivotal role that African American jockeys played in its early years.

Clayton, along with other African American jockeys of his time, left an indelible mark on the sport, even as racial discrimination began to push many of these talented athletes off the tracks.

In addition, Clayton's victory in 1892 was a testament to his skill and determination, overcoming both the challenges of competition and the social barriers of the time.

His feat remains an unbroken record in the history of the Kentucky Derby, and to this day, no jockey has won the race at a younger age.

Lonnie Clayton is part of the rich and often forgotten history of African American jockeys who helped shape the sport of horse racing in the United States.

Although his career was relatively short, his achievement of winning the Derby at 15 years old makes him a legend in the racing world and an example of the importance of diversity in sports, even during times of segregation and racial hardship.

# 21

**The garland of 400 roses is one of the most iconic symbols of the Kentucky Derby, awarded to the winner of the race as part of a tradition that has endured for more than a century.**

This garland, which weighs about 40 pounds (18 kilograms), is made entirely of red roses and is draped over the winning horse at the end of the race during a special ceremony.

Because of this floral tribute, the Kentucky Derby is known as the "Run for the Roses."

The tradition of roses began in 1883, when Meriwether Lewis Clark Jr., the socialite and founder of the Derby, attended an event in Louisville where roses were given to the ladies in attendance.

Inspired by the beauty of the flowers and the symbolism they represented, Clark decided that red roses would be the official symbol of the Derby.

However, it wasn't until 1896 that a garland of roses was first awarded to the winning horse, solidifying this tradition.

The current rose garland is crafted each year by Kroger, a florist that assembles the piece the night before the race.

The process of creating the garland is extremely meticulous and takes several hours.

Each rose is placed by hand, and the garland measures around 2.5 meters (8 feet) in length.

The garland is lined with a green silk ribbon bearing the Kentucky Derby seal, and at the center of the garland is a crown of roses, ferns, and flowers.

The detail that the garland weighs approximately 40 pounds adds a symbolic element of "grandeur" to the recognition, as it not only represents victory but also the weight of the achievement and tradition.

The image of the winning horse draped with the garland over its shoulders is one of the most anticipated and photographed moments of the event, symbolizing the culmination of the Triple Crown dream.

In addition to the garland, the Kentucky Derby has been immortalized in American culture for its focus on elegance and spectacle.

The award ceremony is filled with pomp, with the anthem "My Old Kentucky Home" played at Churchill Downs, while spectators and jockeys celebrate the success of the winning horse.

The nickname "Run for the Roses" has become as famous as the Kentucky Derby itself.

This name not only reflects the prize awarded to the winning horse but also the festive and vibrant atmosphere surrounding the race.

The first Saturday in May, when the Derby is held, is an event rich with symbolism, and the rose garland plays a key role in that narrative.

Over the years, this garland has become an icon of the sport and a reminder of the prestige that accompanies the Derby winner.

# 22

**The Standardbred is a breed of horse known for its versatility and strong ability in harness racing (trot and pace races) where small carts, called sulkies, are pulled by the horse.**

This breed was primarily developed in the United States in the late 19th century and is noted for its endurance, speed, and gentle disposition.

While their main use is for trot and pace racing, Standardbred horses are also used in other equestrian disciplines due to their versatile and calm nature.

The origin of the Standardbred breed lies in the crossing of several breeds, primarily Thoroughbreds, Morgans, and other breeds that are now extinct.

The most influential Thoroughbred in the development of the Standardbred was Messenger, a Thoroughbred imported to the United States in 1788.

Messenger was the ancestor of Hambletonian 10, the most influential horse in the creation of the modern Standardbred breed.

Hambletonian 10, born in 1849, is considered the father of the breed, as his descendants demonstrated a natural ability for fast trotting, making them favorites for harness racing.

The name Standardbred comes from the "standard" used to register horses that were able to trot or pace a mile within a specific time.

This standard was established in 1879, and any horse that could trot a mile in less than 2 minutes and 30 seconds was considered eligible to be registered as a Standardbred.

Over time, the standard has evolved, and today Standardbreds are much faster, with race times often completed in under two minutes.

In addition to their success in trot and pace racing, Standardbreds are also valued for their gentle temperament and calm disposition.

They are very easy to handle, making them an ideal choice for beginner riders or those looking for a reliable working horse.

Standardbred foals are typically easy to train and are not easily spooked, making them well-suited for a variety of equestrian activities.

One of the most notable aspects of the Standardbred breed is its versatility.

Although their primary purpose is for harness racing, these horses can also excel in other disciplines such as jumping, dressage, and pleasure riding.

Many retired Standardbreds find a second career as recreational horses or in competitions in other areas of equestrian sports.

Their ability to adapt to different environments and physical demands makes them highly valued in both sport and recreational riding.

In terms of their physique, Standardbreds are sturdy and

well-built horses.

They have a powerful muscular structure, especially in the legs and chest, providing them with the strength and endurance necessary to maintain high speeds over long periods.

Their height typically ranges from 1.47 to 1.73 meters at the withers, and their weight can vary between 400 and 550 kg.

They have well-proportioned heads with expressive eyes, muscular necks, and strong backs, making them balanced and athletic horses.

In harness racing, Standardbreds compete in two main categories: trotters and pacers.

Trotters move their legs diagonally, meaning the right front leg moves in sync with the left hind leg, and vice versa.

Pacers, on the other hand, move their legs laterally, meaning both legs on the same side move together.

Pacers are generally faster than trotters and make up the majority of the horses competing in harness racing in North America.

In addition to their popularity in the United States and Canada, Standardbreds are also used in Europe, particularly in countries like Sweden, Norway, and France, where trotting races have a long-standing tradition.

In these countries, Standardbreds compete in mounted trotting races, a variation where riders mount the horses directly instead of using a harness or sulky.

The longevity and durability of Standardbred horses are also highly valued traits.

These horses often have long, productive careers and can compete at a high level for several years, increasing their value both on and off the track.

Their endurance and ability to recover from intense exertion make them one of the toughest breeds in equestrian competitions.

# 23

**Money wagered on horse racing by country.**

**1. United States:** Horse racing bets in the U.S. generate over $11 billion annually. The Kentucky Derby is one of the biggest betting events in the country, moving around $200 million just for that event each year.

**2. United Kingdom:** Horse racing in the UK is a multi-billion-pound industry, with betting on races generating an estimated £14 billion annually. Events like the Royal Ascot and Grand National are the biggest in terms of betting, attracting both local and international bettors.

**3. Japan:** Japan is one of the countries where the most money is wagered on horse racing, with annual betting revenues exceeding $20 billion. The Japan Cup is one of the world's most important horse racing events, with a massive amount of money wagered.

**4. Australia:** Horse racing bets in Australia generate more than A$30 billion annually. The Melbourne Cup, considered "the race that stops a nation," is the main betting event in the country, with billions wagered each year.

**5. France:** Turf betting generates around €10 billion annually, with major events like the Prix de l'Arc de Triomphe drawing the bulk of the bets.

**6. Argentina:** In Argentina, horse racing is an important part of sports culture, with betting moving around $800 million annually.

The Gran Premio Nacional and Gran Premio Carlos Pellegrini are the most important events in terms of betting.

**7. Brazil:** Brazil also has a strong horse racing tradition, with bets generating around $600 million annually. The Grande Prêmio Brasil is one of the standout events.

**8. Chile:** In Chile, horse racing bets move about $300 million annually, with the Clásico El Ensayo being the most important event.

**9. Uruguay:** In Uruguay, horse racing generates around $100 million annually in betting, with the Gran Premio Ramírez as the main event.

**10. South Africa:** In South Africa, horse racing bets exceed 2 billion rand annually. The most prominent event is the Durban July, which generates a significant amount of betting each year.

**11. Ireland:** Ireland has a rich horse racing tradition, and betting on horse races is a key part of its culture. Horse racing bets in Ireland generate around €1 billion annually. Racecourses like Curragh and events like the Irish Derby and Cheltenham Festival (though held in the UK, many Irish horses and bettors participate) are popular both nationally and internationally.

**12. Hong Kong:** Although it is a special administrative region of China, Hong Kong is one of the leading horse racing betting centers in the world. The Hong Kong Jockey Club is the only organization authorized to manage race betting, moving over $13 billion annually in bets. Races like the Hong Kong Derby and the Hong Kong Cup attract both local and international bettors, cementing Hong Kong as a major global hub for horse racing.

# 24

**The diet of racehorses is a crucial factor for both their performance on the track and their overall health and well-being.**

These horses have specific nutritional needs due to the intense physical activity they undergo.

A proper diet not only enhances their endurance and energy but also aids in muscle recovery, digestive health, and the strength of their bones and tendons.

The foundation of a racehorse's diet is primarily made up of forage or fiber, which is essential for their digestive system.

Forage is the main component of equine nutrition because horses have a digestive system designed to consume large amounts of fiber throughout the day.

The most common type of forage is grass hay, with Timothy hay being one of the most popular choices.

This type of hay is valued for its high quality and digestibility, providing fiber that keeps the digestive system functioning properly, helps prevent gastrointestinal issues like colic, and ensures a sustained release of energy.

In addition to grass hay, many trainers incorporate alfalfa into the diet of racehorses.

Alfalfa is a legume rich in protein, calcium, and vitamins, which contribute to the development and maintenance of muscle mass.

Since racehorses require a significant amount of protein to repair and build muscles after training sessions and races, alfalfa becomes a key component.

It is also beneficial because it is more nutrient-dense than other types of forage, allowing horses to gain more energy from a smaller quantity of food.

The combination of grass hay and alfalfa provides an ideal balance of fiber and protein, essential elements for horses in constant training.

While grass hay provides steady energy through fiber, alfalfa adds the necessary protein component for muscle recovery.

This also helps maintain the horse's physical condition, allowing it to be in top shape during competitions.

In addition to forage, many trainers include concentrates or grains in the diet of racehorses.

Concentrates typically include oats, barley, corn, or specially formulated commercial feeds for high-performance horses.

These foods provide extra energy in the form of carbohydrates and fats, which are necessary to meet the energy demands of intense training and races.

However, it is crucial that these grains are balanced with fiber, as excessive grain intake without enough fiber can cause digestive issues.

Another essential component in the diet of racehorses is the supplementation of vitamins and minerals.

Since racehorses sweat a lot during training and races, it's essential to replenish lost electrolytes such as sodium, potassium, and chloride.

Electrolyte supplements are often added to their diet, especially during hot months or before major competitions.

These supplements ensure that horses maintain the proper electrolyte balance, preventing dehydration and improving their ability to perform at their best.

In addition to electrolytes, trainers may also include specific supplements to support joint health, muscle recovery, and the horse's immune system.

Glucosamine, chondroitin, and hyaluronic acid supplements are popular for maintaining joint health, especially in horses subjected to extreme physical exertion.

On the other hand, omega-3 fatty acids, which can come from sources like flaxseed oil or fish oil, help reduce inflammation and promote muscle recovery.

Water is another crucial factor in the diet of racehorses.

A racehorse can consume up to 40-50 liters of water per day, depending on the climate and the intensity of exercise.

Proper hydration is essential for maintaining the horse's overall health, aiding in body temperature regulation, digestion, and blood circulation.

Additionally, water plays a key role in nutrient absorption.

Another important aspect of feeding is managing the meal schedule.

Trainers usually feed horses in small, frequent portions throughout the day rather than giving them large amounts of food at once.

This is because horses have relatively small stomachs and are designed to graze continuously throughout the day.

Dividing feed into multiple meals helps prevent overloading the digestive system and reduces the risk of issues like colic or obesity.

Proper feeding care also includes managing the horse's body weight.

Trainers and veterinarians closely monitor the horse's body condition, ensuring it is neither too thin nor too heavy, as both extremes can negatively affect performance.

A horse that is underweight may lack energy and stamina, while an overweight horse may be more prone to joint injuries and other health problems.

# 25

**The equine world on the racetrack is a universe full of surprising revelations, where the behavior, intelligence, and emotional connection between horses and jockeys unfold in fascinating ways in every race.**

Racetracks are not just a stage for exciting competitions but also a laboratory where complex patterns of interaction and performance are observed, revealing just how capable these animals are of adapting to and understanding their environment, beyond what was previously thought.

Recent observations have revealed that horses possess an astonishing ability to anticipate the outcome of races.

They don't just react instinctively but seem to analyze and process information from their surroundings, such as the speed of other horses, their position on the track, and the physical condition of their competitors.

This anticipatory ability is a form of advanced instinct that shows horses are not merely following orders, but are active participants in the dynamics of the race.

Based on strategies developed during training and their own intuition, horses are able to adjust their performance, deciding when to accelerate or conserve energy, which has impressed experts in the field.

Another significant development in the world of racing is the use of advanced technology to improve the understanding and performance of horses on the track.

Trainers now use tracking and data analysis equipment, such as GPS devices, sensors, and specialized software, to monitor in detail the movement, speed, and race strategies of horses.

These devices allow for the collection of precise information about how a horse moves during different stages of the race, detecting patterns of efficiency or weak points that might have gone unnoticed before.

For example, they can identify changes in a horse's posture or balance that could be affecting its speed or its ability to maintain a steady pace.

Thanks to these advancements, trainers can adjust training programs to maximize the horse's performance, improving its responsiveness on the track.

These technological advancements have also enhanced the experience for fans.

Today, turf enthusiasts can access real-time data analysis, allowing them to view races from a completely new perspective.

It's no longer just about watching the competition, but about understanding the nuances of each horse's performance: how they manage their energy, how they interact with other competitors, and how they adjust their pace throughout the race.

This information has transformed casual observation into a detail-rich experience, where every step and movement holds strategic significance that fans can interpret.

But undoubtedly, one of the most important aspects of a horse's performance on the track is the connection between rider and horse.

This relationship is based on perfect synchronization and non-verbal communication, which are crucial for success in a race.

Horses, being incredibly perceptive animals, can read the emotions and moods of their riders.

Recent studies have shown that horses can detect subtle changes in posture, muscle tone, or even the rider's breathing, allowing them to respond in real-time to the intentions of their rider.

This ability to perceive and respond to the emotional and physical cues of the rider highlights the importance of a relationship built on trust and empathy.

The emotional management of the rider is essential, as horses are highly sensitive to the confidence or nervousness they sense.

A rider who projects calm and confidence can help the horse stay composed in high-pressure situations, while one who displays anxiety may trigger erratic behavior in the animal.

This empathy between horse and rider forms the foundation of effective communication on the track.

In fact, a simple adjustment in posture or a light touch can be enough for the horse to understand what is expected of it.

This reinforces the idea that riders must guide and correct the horse with gentleness, as a harsh or insensitive approach could break the synchronization and negatively impact performance.

On a physical level, horses also develop an impressive capacity for learning.

Over the course of multiple races, horses not only adapt to different racing styles and track conditions, but they also learn from their experiences.

They can remember race patterns, how other horses reacted in similar situations, and adjust their approach in future competitions.

This type of adaptive intelligence has surprised both trainers and scientists, demonstrating that horses have a high level of memory and decision-making ability.

Another fascinating aspect on the track is the importance of leadership among horses.

Some horses develop a dominant attitude during the race, taking control of the group and setting the pace.

This kind of behavior is common in situations where horses run in large groups, and the natural leadership of some of them can influence how the race unfolds.

These dominant horses are capable of setting a race pace that others follow, giving them a strategic advantage, as they can conserve energy while dictating the flow of the competition.

# 26

**The jockey is a key figure in the world of horse racing, and their role goes far beyond simply riding the horse during the competition.**

Jockeys are highly trained professional athletes who must meet strict physical and technical requirements to compete at the highest level.

In order to perform their job in horse racing, jockeys must obtain an official license, which certifies that they are qualified and meet the regulations set by the horse racing authorities in each country or jurisdiction.

The jockey's license is a fundamental requirement for participating in official races, and it is obtained after a training process that includes both physical conditioning and technical knowledge of race rules, riding skills, and the ability to work with horses.

Additionally, if a jockey wishes to become a horse owner or trainer, they must acquire a trainer's license, which requires meeting more specific requirements, both in terms of education and experience in managing and training racehorses.

Many jockeys, after retiring from competition, choose to become trainers, leveraging their knowledge and experience in the sport.

One of the most distinctive characteristics of jockeys is their physique, as they must maintain an extremely low body weight to minimize the load on the horse during the race.

This is because, in the world of horse racing, the weight-to-speed ratio is critical.

Racehorses perform better when carrying less weight, allowing them to reach higher speeds and maintain more stamina during the race.

As a result, jockeys tend to be short-statured individuals, with an average height of around 1.50 meters (5 feet), and they maintain a body weight between 48 and 50 kilograms (105-110 pounds).

This combination of height and weight enables jockeys to optimize the horse's performance without overburdening it.

The jockey's weight is so important that they are weighed both before and after the race.

Before each race, jockeys must step on a scale to ensure they meet the regulatory weight assigned to each horse.

This weight includes not only the jockey's body weight but also their equipment, such as the saddle, helmet, and other protective gear.

After the race, jockeys are weighed again to verify that they haven't lost significant weight during the race, which could have altered the conditions of the competition.

This process is crucial to ensure that races are conducted fairly and equitably, and any deviation in weight could result in penalties.

To maintain their weight, jockeys often follow strict diet and exercise routines.

Many jockeys have to follow very strict diets, often significantly reducing their caloric intake before a race to ensure they meet the weight limits.

Some even resort to techniques like spending time in saunas to shed additional body water.

This strict weight control can have health consequences for jockeys, so many also need to carefully balance their nutrition to stay strong and energetic.

In terms of physical preparation, jockeys require a high level of endurance, strength, and balance.

Although the horses do the main physical work in the race, jockeys need to be extremely agile and capable of controlling the horse with subtle and precise movements.

The posture they maintain during the race, leaning forward and slightly suspended over the horse, demands significant leg and core strength, as well as excellent coordination.

Additionally, they must be able to react quickly to the horse's changes in pace or unexpected situations on the track, making their task both a physical and mental challenge.

Jockeys must also possess great tactical ability.

During the race, they are responsible for making crucial decisions in a matter of seconds: when to accelerate, when to hold the horse back, when to attempt overtaking other competitors, and how to navigate through the other horses on the track.

This decision-making, based on knowledge of the horse, experience on the track, and intuition acquired over the course of their career, is what often sets successful jockeys apart from the rest.

# 27

**Horseback races without saddles, also known as bareback racing, are a type of equestrian competition in which riders mount horses without using a saddle or other common equipment like stirrups or girths.**

In this style of racing, riders must rely solely on their balance and ability to control the horse by using their body weight, legs, and hands directly on the horse's back.

These races are more challenging than traditional ones due to the lack of equipment that aids in stability and control.

Bareback races have their roots in ancient times, when early civilizations rode horses without the use of sophisticated saddles.

At that time, it was the only way to ride before modern saddles were invented.

Although the use of saddles became widespread over the centuries to improve control and comfort for both rider and horse, bareback racing continued in some cultures as a testament to the skill and dexterity of the riders.

Today, bareback races are primarily held in traditional or cultural contexts and are less common than saddle races in official competitions.

A notable example of these races is the Palio di Siena in Italy, one of the most famous bareback competitions in the world.

Held twice a year in the city of Siena, the Palio is a race dating back to the Middle Ages, where riders compete without a saddle on a circuit that surrounds the Piazza del Campo, a square in the center of the city.

This race is particularly dangerous due to the narrow layout and sharp turns of the course, which require great skill from the riders.

Bareback races have also been held in some indigenous communities in North America and other parts of the world, where riding in this manner is part of the local equestrian tradition.

Native Americans, for example, were known for riding bareback and having masterful control over their horses, which allowed them to use this technique not only in races but also in their hunting and warfare tactics.

In terms of difficulty, bareback racing demands a significant amount of balance, strength, and endurance from the rider.

Without a saddle to provide stability, riders must learn to adjust to the horse's movements, which involves constant use of core, leg, and upper body muscles.

Additionally, the lack of stirrups, which in traditional races help the rider to push off and maintain stability, means that bareback riders must use their legs more effectively to hold on and communicate with the horse.

Communication with the horse also changes in bareback racing, since, without the same control elements used in traditional races, such as reins and stirrups, the rider relies heavily on leg pressure and direct contact with the horse's back to guide it.

This more direct communication between the rider and the horse creates a closer connection, as the rider must be more intuitively attuned to the horse's natural movements.

Additionally, bareback racing tends to be more dangerous than traditional racing due to the higher possibility of falls or loss of control of the horse.

Without a saddle, the rider has nothing to stabilize them in situations where the horse makes sudden or unexpected movements, increasing the risk of injury.

For this reason, bareback racing is often seen as a high-risk discipline that tests the rider's skill, courage, and ability in an extreme way.

In terms of training, riders who compete in bareback races must regularly practice to strengthen their ability to stay balanced and centered on the horse's back without the support of a saddle.

This involves not only physical training but also a deep understanding of the horse's behavior and way of moving.

The horse also needs to be trained to respond to the subtle signals the rider gives through body pressure and leg cues.

In some more modern sporting events, such as rodeos, bareback riding is also practiced, although typically in the context of events like bareback bronc riding, where riders must stay on a horse that is trying to buck them off without the use of a saddle.

However, this type of riding is more of a test of endurance and staying power.

# 28

**Notable movies and series about horse racing.**

**1. Seabiscuit (2003):** This is one of the most iconic films about horse racing, based on the true story of the famous racehorse that became a symbol of hope during the Great Depression. Starring Tobey Maguire, Jeff Bridges, and Chris Cooper, the movie tells how Seabiscuit, an unconventional horse, exceeded expectations and became a sports icon. The story focuses on the bond between the horse, his jockey, owner, and trainer, who all strive to overcome their own personal obstacles. The film was a critical and box office success, earning multiple Academy Award nominations.

**2. Secretariat (2010):** This film tells the story of one of the greatest horses in racing history, the winner of the Triple Crown in 1973. Starring Diane Lane as Penny Chenery, Secretariat's owner, and John Malkovich as the trainer, the movie follows the legendary horse and his historic Triple Crown run, culminating in his incredible victory at the Belmont Stakes, where he won by one of the largest margins in the sport's history. The film is both a celebration of the horse and a look at the horse racing world through themes of perseverance and courage.

**3. Dreamer (2005):** Based on the story of Mariah's Storm, a horse that returned to the track after a serious injury, "Dreamer" stars Kurt Russell and Dakota Fanning. The story revolves around a horse trainer and his daughter as they try to rehabilitate an injured horse in the hopes of returning it to competitive racing.

Unlike other films in the genre, "Dreamer" focuses on family relationships and hope, and how a love for horses can be a unifying force.

**4. Phar Lap (1983):** This Australian film tells the story of Phar Lap, one of the most successful and beloved racehorses in Australia and New Zealand during the 1930s. The film explores not only Phar Lap's success on the racetrack but also the financial and personal struggles faced by his trainer and jockey. The horse tragically died under suspicious circumstances, adding an element of mystery and tragedy to the story. "Phar Lap" has become a classic in horse racing cinema.

**5. Ruffian (2007):** This film tells the story of one of the most famous fillies in U.S. horse racing history. Ruffian dominated the racetrack until she suffered a tragic injury in 1975 during a race. Starring Sam Shepard, the movie focuses on her speed, determination, and the tragic end of her career. Ruffian is remembered as one of the greatest female racehorses, and the film pays tribute to her legacy.

**6. National Velvet (1944):** Starring a young Elizabeth Taylor, this is one of the most beloved films about horses and racing. The story follows a girl who dreams of training a horse to win the Grand National, the famous British race. Although the film is more about personal triumph and dreams fulfilled, it remains one of the most iconic classics in horse racing cinema. It was a critical and commercial success and helped launch Elizabeth Taylor's career.

**7. Luck (2011-2012):** This HBO series, starring Dustin Hoffman and Nick Nolte, offers a deep and realistic look into the world of horse racing. The series follows the lives of several characters, including owners, jockeys, trainers, and bettors, all connected by their love and ambition in the world of horse racing.

Although the series was praised for its realistic portrayal of the racing world, it was canceled after one season due to concerns over horse safety. Nonetheless, it remains an important reference in the genre.

**8. The Black Stallion (1979):** This film tells the story of a young boy and a wild horse who survive a shipwreck and form a deep bond. The second half of the film focuses on horse racing, as the boy decides to train the horse to compete in a major race. This movie combines elements of adventure and drama and is considered one of the most beautifully filmed horse movies.

**9. 50 to 1 (2014):** Based on the true story of Mine That Bird, the 2009 Kentucky Derby winner, "50 to 1" follows an unlikely group of friends who take a seemingly underdog horse to victory in one of the world's most important races. The film portrays both the challenges and joys of competing in the world of horse racing, and it's a story of overcoming obstacles and teamwork.

**10. "Let It Ride" (1989):** This comedy, starring Richard Dreyfuss, offers a fun look at horse racing from the perspective of a bettor. The film follows a man who, after receiving a hot tip on a race, experiences a day of incredible luck at the racetrack and can't stop winning. As his good fortune continues, the comedy unfolds as he wrestles with the temptation to keep betting and the chaos that ensues. While this movie leans more into comedy than the drama of racing, it remains a classic for horse racing fans who love the thrill of betting and the vibrant atmosphere of the racetrack.

# 29

**Deaths and serious accidents of famous jockeys.**

**1. Frank Hayes (1923):** One of the most unusual and tragic cases in horse racing history was that of Frank Hayes, an American jockey who died in 1923 while riding the horse Sweet Kiss at Belmont Park in New York. What makes this accident particularly remarkable is that Hayes won the race, but passed away during the competition. Apparently, Hayes suffered a heart attack while racing, but his body remained on the horse until they crossed the finish line. He was declared dead after the race, making this a unique case in which a jockey died during a race but the horse still won. This incident remains one of the most bizarre and sad accidents in the history of the sport.

**2. José Flores (2018):** José Flores, one of the most experienced and successful jockeys in U.S. racetracks, died in 2018 following an accident at Parx Racing in Pennsylvania. During a race, the horse he was riding, Love Rules, stumbled just before the finish line, causing Flores to fall violently. Despite wearing protective gear, Flores sustained head and neck injuries. Although he was rushed to the hospital, the injuries proved fatal, and he passed away a few days later. Flores was highly respected within the jockey community, with more than 4,600 wins in his career, making his death a particularly devastating blow to the horse racing world.

**3. Timber Wolkotte (1976):** An American jockey, Wolkotte suffered a serious accident in 1976 during a race at River Downs in Cincinnati. During the competition, his horse, Bet's Gambit, stumbled and fell, causing Wolkotte to be thrown to the ground.

He was trampled by several horses coming from behind, resulting in devastating injuries. Although he did not die at the time of the accident, his injuries were so severe that he had to retire from the sport and was left with permanent disabilities. This accident highlighted the vulnerability of jockeys in large-scale falls and the dangers they face when multiple horses are moving at high speeds.

**4. Chris Antley (1999):** A highly successful American jockey, winner of the Kentucky Derby twice (1991 and 1999), had a career full of highs and lows and a tragic end. Although Antley did not die on the racetrack, he suffered numerous falls throughout his career, many of which resulted in serious injuries. He temporarily retired due to substance abuse issues, but returned in 1999 and won the Derby riding Charismatic. However, later that same year during the Belmont Stakes, Charismatic was seriously injured, and Antley heroically jumped off immediately to hold the horse's leg until the veterinarians arrived, preventing further injury. In December 1999, Antley was found dead at his home under suspicious circumstances. Although his death did not occur on the track, his life was marked by accidents and challenges related to his career as a jockey.

**5. Apprentice Thomas Burrill (2015):** The young jockey Thomas Burrill, known as an apprentice, suffered a fatal accident in 2015 at Ellis Park Race Course in Kentucky. While riding the horse Freaky Kiki, the animal unexpectedly fell, causing Burrill to be thrown from the horse. He was tossed to the ground and left in a vulnerable position, where he was trampled by other horses coming from behind. The head and chest injuries he sustained were fatal, despite wearing a helmet and protective gear. His death was a harsh reminder of the dangers jockeys face, especially those just starting their careers.

**6. Ralph Neves (1936):** Known for his bravery and aggressive style on the racetrack, Neves was involved in an incident that seemed fatal but had an unexpected outcome. In 1936, during a race at Bay Meadows Racetrack, Neves was thrown from his horse and hit his head so hard that he was declared dead on the spot. However, shortly after being taken to the morgue, Neves woke up. Not only did he survive the accident, but after recovering, he returned to the track that same day and rode in another race. This incident, while not ending in death, demonstrated the tenacity and risks jockeys face, even when situations seem to be life-threatening.

**7. George Woolf (1946):** Known as "The Iceman," Woolf was one of the most prominent jockeys of his time, famous for riding Seabiscuit in his legendary race against War Admiral in 1938. Woolf suffered a fatal accident in 1946 during a race at Santa Anita Park. During the race, Woolf lost control of his horse, and it is speculated that he may have fainted or experienced a physical problem before the fall. He was violently thrown to the ground and suffered a skull fracture that proved to be fatal. Woolf is remembered as one of the greatest jockeys of his era, and his death shocked the racing world.

**8. Kieren Kelly (2003):** The Irish jockey tragically died in 2003 following an accident during a hurdles race at Kilbeggan Racecourse in Ireland. Kelly fell while riding his horse Baltiman, who stumbled at one of the jumps. The fall was extremely violent, and Kelly sustained fatal head injuries. Although he was rushed to the hospital, he could not recover. This accident was especially sad, as Kelly was considered one of the most promising jockeys in the Irish hurdles racing scene.

**9. Roger Blanc (1962):** The French jockey lost his life during a race in 1962 when his horse, Lettre Brune, stumbled and fell.

Blanc was thrown to the ground and trampled by other horses on the track, causing severe internal injuries. Although he was quickly taken to the hospital, he died shortly after due to the severity of his injuries. This accident shocked the French equestrian community and highlighted the ever-present risks in the sport.

**10. Freddy Tett (2017):** This young and talented amateur jockey suffered a serious accident in 2017 during a race at Larkhill, UK. During the competition, his horse, Colonel Frank, fell, and Tett was thrown to the ground, where he was trampled on the head and chest. Although he was airlifted to the hospital and underwent emergency surgery, the injuries to his head and neck were severe. Freddy survived, but his career as a jockey was affected by the lasting consequences of the accident.

**11. Mark "Jacko" Jackson (2004):** The Australian jockey tragically died in 2004 during a race at Taree Racecourse, New South Wales. While riding the horse Russian Charm, Jackson lost control and fell off his mount. During the fall, he suffered a blow to the head that resulted in a fatal brain injury. Although he was rushed to the hospital, the injuries were too severe, and he passed away shortly after the accident. This incident shocked the Australian horse racing community and once again highlighted the inherent dangers of the sport.

**12. Crispin Freeman (1993):** The British jockey died in 1993 following an accident at Southwell Racecourse, UK. Freeman was riding Dancing Bloom when his horse stumbled and fell, causing Freeman to be violently thrown to the ground. Unfortunately, he was trampled by another horse coming from behind. Despite being rushed to the hospital, the internal injuries were so severe that he did not survive. Crispin Freeman was a talented jockey, and his death was a significant loss for the British equestrian community.

# 30

**Elite jockey salaries.**

Jockey earnings can vary significantly depending on various factors, such as geographic location, level of competition, races won, prize purses, and sponsorships.

Elite jockeys in prestigious events like the Kentucky Derby, the Triple Crown, the Prix de l'Arc de Triomphe, and other major international races can earn substantial sums of money, while jockeys at lower levels tend to earn much less.

The income model for jockeys is primarily based on commissions for each race they participate in.

A jockey charges a standard fee simply for riding in a race, which typically ranges from $30 to $150 USD per race, depending on the country and the level of competition.

However, the significant earnings come from commissions on race winnings.

When a jockey wins a race, they usually receive around 10% of the prize purse of the winning horse.

If the horse finishes in second or third place, the percentage decreases, typically around 5% or 3% of the winnings.

While the prize money may seem small in local races, in major competitions where purses can reach millions of dollars, the jockey's commissions increase significantly.

**1. Mike Smith:** He is one of the most famous and successful jockeys in horse racing history, known for winning the Triple Crown in 2018 riding Justify. Throughout his career, Smith has accumulated over $330 million USD in earnings, placing him among the richest jockeys in history. Although the total winnings include the prizes earned for the owners, the 10% he receives has allowed him to build a considerable fortune. Additionally, with his participation in high-profile events like the Breeders' Cup and the Kentucky Derby, his career has been highly lucrative.

**2. Frankie Dettori:** The Italian jockey is another big name in the world of horse racing. Dettori has won multiple major races in Europe and America, including several titles in the Prix de l'Arc de Triomphe and the Ascot Gold Cup. His total earnings are estimated to exceed $210 million USD. Dettori is also known for his sponsorship deals and commercial agreements with major brands, which further increase his income.

**3. John Velazquez:** The Puerto Rican jockey has been one of the most prominent jockeys in the United States, winning multiple Kentucky Derbies and Breeders' Cup races. Over his career, Velazquez has amassed more than $450 million USD in winnings. Like other elite jockeys, his share of the prize purses has allowed him to accumulate a significant fortune, with annual salaries easily exceeding millions of dollars in his most successful seasons.

**4. Laffit Pincay Jr.:** Considered one of the greatest jockeys of all time, Pincay earned over $237 million USD in winnings before retiring in 2003. Despite retiring two decades ago, he remains a benchmark for consistency and long-term success, demonstrating how horse racing can be incredibly lucrative for jockeys who reach the top.

**5. Ryan Moore:** A highly successful British jockey, Moore is considered one of the best on the international racing circuit. With victories in prestigious races such as the Epsom Derby, the Prix de l'Arc de Triomphe, and multiple titles at Royal Ascot, Moore has earned considerable winnings. It is estimated that he has earned over $300 million USD in prize money throughout his career, with around 10% coming from the prize purses of the races he has won. As the primary jockey for Aidan O'Brien's stables, one of the world's most successful trainers, Moore regularly has access to top-tier horses, significantly boosting his earnings.

**6. Javier Castellano:** The Venezuelan jockey has had a highly successful career in the United States, with major wins in events like the Preakness Stakes, the Belmont Stakes, and multiple editions of the Breeders' Cup. Throughout his career, Castellano has earned over $380 million USD in prize money, placing him among the richest and most successful jockeys of recent decades. His annual earnings often exceed $5 million USD, and he is known for his consistency on the U.S. racing circuit.

**7. Joel Rosario:** The Dominican jockey has earned over $260 million USD in prize money during his career in the U.S., highlighted by victories in the Breeders' Cup and the Kentucky Derby with Orb in 2013. Rosario has been one of the most consistent jockeys in terms of high-level wins, allowing him to generate substantial annual income. In standout years, his earnings can easily exceed $10 million USD, particularly considering his participation in top-tier races.

**8. Pat Day:** The American jockey is another of the most successful in U.S. racing history. Over his career, Day accumulated more than $298 million USD in prize money before retiring in 2005.

Winner of a Kentucky Derby and multiple editions of the Breeders' Cup, Pat Day is a legend in horse racing. At his peak, he could earn several million dollars per year, thanks to his skill in winning major races and his consistency on the track.

**9. Jerry Bailey:** Another celebrated jockey on the U.S. circuit, Bailey accumulated more than $296 million USD in winnings during his career. He is known for winning two Kentucky Derbies and five Breeders' Cup Classics and for being one of the most reliable jockeys in major competitions. In addition to prize money, Bailey served as a brand ambassador for several companies, further boosting his earnings. He retired in 2006 and remains a key figure in horse racing analysis and coverage.

**10. Garrett Gomez:** The American jockey was one of the best of his generation, amassing over $205 million USD in prize money throughout his career. Gomez is remembered for his success in the Breeders' Cup, where he won multiple races. Though his career was marked by personal challenges, his talent and success on the track made him one of the highest-paid jockeys of his time, with annual earnings often exceeding $5 million USD.

**11. Bill Shoemaker:** Considered a legend of U.S. horse racing, Shoemaker accumulated over $123 million USD in prize money over his career—an impressive achievement, considering that much of his career took place in earlier decades when prize purses were not as large as they are today. Shoemaker won 11 Triple Crown races and was one of the most successful jockeys of all time. While his annual earnings varied throughout the years, his victories and longevity in the sport allowed him to amass a considerable fortune.

**12. Victor Espinoza:** A Mexican jockey, Espinoza is best

known for winning the Triple Crown in 2015 with American Pharoah. Victor Espinoza has accumulated over $206 million USD in prize money throughout his career, with multiple victories in the Kentucky Derby, Preakness Stakes, and Belmont Stakes. His wins in such prestigious races have easily pushed his annual earnings into the millions during successful seasons, and he also generates additional income through sponsorships and commercial deals.

**13. Willie Shoemaker:** Another legendary jockey in the United States, Shoemaker was one of the best over several decades. He amassed more than $123 million USD in winnings before retiring in 1990. He won the Kentucky Derby four times, as well as other major races like the Belmont Stakes and the Preakness Stakes. His longevity in the sport, combined with his natural talent for big races, allowed him to earn a fortune throughout his career.

**14. Yutaka Take:** One of the most successful and recognized jockeys globally, Take has had a standout career both in Japan and in international competitions. He has amassed over $950 million USD in prize money throughout his career, making him one of the richest jockeys of all time. In Japan, prize purses are substantial, and Yutaka Take has been one of the greatest beneficiaries of this. His ability to win major races, such as the Japan Cup, has cemented his position as one of the highest-paid jockeys in history.

# 31

**Complex tactics used in horse racing around the world.**

**1. The "Energy Conservation" Tactic – United States.**
One of the most common tactics in the U.S., especially in long races like the Kentucky Derby or the Belmont Stakes, is the "energy conservation" strategy. In this tactic, the jockey keeps the horse in a mid-pack or rear position for most of the race, allowing the horse to conserve its energy. Jockeys who use this tactic aim to prevent the horse from expending too much effort in the early stages, keeping it relaxed and controlled so that it has the necessary strength for a strong finish in the final phase.

**-Advantages:** This tactic allows the horse to have enough energy for a strong push in the final stretch. It is particularly effective in long races, where front-runners tend to tire out.

**-Disadvantages:** The risk of this tactic is that the horse may get stuck in the middle of the pack or may not find enough space to make its final move. Additionally, if other horses accelerate early, it can be difficult to catch up.

**2. Pace Control – United Kingdom.**
In British races, especially over long distances like the Grand National or races at tracks like Ascot, a key tactic is pace control. Here, the jockey's task is to set a steady pace to prevent the horse from using up its energy too quickly. Often, the jockey using this tactic positions the horse near the front, but not necessarily leading, ensuring that the horse remains comfortable and in rhythm.

**-Advantages:** Maintaining a steady pace helps prevent the horse from tiring prematurely and allows it to save energy for the final stretch of the race. It also allows the jockey to adjust according to the movements of other competitors.

**-Disadvantages:** If the jockey loses control of the pace or succumbs to the pressure from other competitors, the horse may lose its ideal rhythm and tire out too soon.

### 3. The "Pace Setter" or "Rabbit" Tactic – France.

In France, an interesting tactic often used is the employment of a "pace setter" or "rabbit." This strategy involves using a faster horse to take the lead early and set a high pace from the start, forcing other horses to keep up. This horse is not meant to win the race but to tire out the competitors, allowing the stable's main horse, staying in the back, to conserve energy and take the lead in the final meters.

**-Advantages:** This tactic can disrupt the competitors by forcing them to expend more energy than they want to. The main horse can then capitalize on the final phase of the race when others are fatigued.

**-Disadvantages:** If the pace setter fails to establish a sufficiently fast pace, it may not have the desired effect and could allow other horses to manage their energy better. Additionally, sacrificing a horse for this tactic can be costly.

### 4. Early Attack – Japan.

In Japan, where races like the Japan Cup are incredibly popular, one frequently used tactic is the early attack. In this strategy, the jockey makes an aggressive move in the middle phase of the race, rather than waiting until the end. By doing so, the jockey hopes to disorient other competitors and force them to quickly adjust their strategies.

**-Advantages:** This tactic can surprise competitors who are waiting to make their move in the final stretch. Additionally, if the horse gains a significant lead, it can be difficult for others to catch up once it has established a large gap.

**-Disadvantages:** Attacking too early can result in premature exhaustion for the horse. If it lacks the necessary stamina, it is likely to run out of energy in the final meters and be overtaken by the other horses.

## 5. Group or Block Racing – Australia.

In Australia, especially in races like the Melbourne Cup, trainers often prepare their horses to run in groups or blocks, meaning that several horses from the same stable or team collaborate during the race. The jockeys of these horses coordinate their movements to protect their strongest horse, allowing it to conserve energy or avoid getting boxed in by competitors.

**-Advantages:** Group racing can shield a horse from early attacks by competitors, helping it stay well-positioned until the end of the race. Additionally, horses from the same team can block competitors trying to overtake.

**-Disadvantages:** This tactic requires perfect coordination between the jockeys and their horses. If one of the team's horses fails to maintain the pace, it could harm the entire group.

## 6. "Tailwind Advantage" Tactic – Hong Kong.

In Hong Kong, where horse racing is an extremely popular sport, weather conditions play an important role in jockey strategy. A tactic used is to take advantage of tailwinds at certain points in the race.

Jockeys adjust their position on the track based on the wind direction, using tailwinds to increase the horse's speed at key moments in the race.

**-Advantages:** Taking advantage of a tailwind can provide a significant speed boost, allowing the horse to gain ground without expending as much energy.

**-Disadvantages:** Weather conditions are unpredictable, and the wind may change direction, negating the advantage of this tactic. Additionally, other competitors may attempt the same strategy, increasing the competition for position.

**7. The "Late Whip" Tactic – United States and Europe.**
The use of the whip is a controversial but often employed tactic in horse racing to increase the horse's effort in the final meters. This tactic involves using the whip strategically in the last 100-200 meters of the race, encouraging the horse to make one last push.

**-Advantages:** When used correctly, the whip can help the horse release a burst of energy in the final moments, which can be the difference between winning and coming in second.

**-Disadvantages:** Excessive use of the whip is regulated and can result in penalties for the jockey. Additionally, if used too early, it may exhaust the horse before reaching the finish line.

# 32

**Famous jockeys known for their ability
to deceive competitors.**

### 1. Lester Piggott – "False Acceleration":
Lester Piggott, one of the most successful jockeys in history, was a master of tactical deception. One of his most famous tricks was false acceleration, where he would pretend to accelerate in the final stretch, tricking other jockeys into speeding up prematurely. By doing this, Piggott conserved his horse's energy, allowing it to make a final push after the other horses had tired out.

**Notable case:** In one of his most memorable races, Piggott used this tactic in the Epsom Derby, making other jockeys believe he had launched his horse too early. When the other horses began to slow down, Piggott launched his true attack and won the race.

### 2. Mike Smith – "Staying Hidden":
American jockey Mike Smith is famous for his ability to hide his horse's true speed until the last moment. In many races, Smith has positioned himself in the middle or back of the group, ensuring that the other jockeys don't perceive the real potential of his horse. Only in the final meters does he launch a surprise attack, leaving his rivals with no time to react.

**Notable case:** In his victory in the 2009 Breeders' Cup Classic with Zenyatta, Smith kept Zenyatta at the back of the pack for almost the entire race, and in the last 400 meters, he made a stunning charge that took all the other jockeys by surprise.

### 3. Frankie Dettori – "Late Attack":

Italian jockey Frankie Dettori is known for his late attack technique, where he waits until the last seconds of the race to unleash his horse's full power. Dettori often gives the impression that he's out of contention, causing other jockeys to relax, but just in the final 100-200 meters, he makes his move, leaving his rivals with no time to react.

**Notable case:** Dettori used this tactic with great success in the 2015 Prix de l'Arc de Triomphe with Golden Horn, where he appeared to be beaten in the final stretch, but launched a fierce attack in the last meters to win the race.

### 4. Pat Day – "Feigning Fatigue":

American jockey Pat Day was known for his tactic of feigning fatigue. During the race, Day often made it look like both he and his horse were struggling to keep up, causing other jockeys to underestimate their ability. However, at crucial moments, Day and his horse would find a reserve of energy to overtake their rivals.

**Notable case:** This technique was key to his victory in the 1994 Preakness Stakes, when many thought Day had fallen out of the race, only to see him make a dramatic comeback in the final moments.

### 5. John Velazquez – "Hiding the True Position":

John Velazquez, one of the most successful jockeys in the U.S., is known for his ability to conceal his horse's true position. Velazquez often keeps his horse in a middle position, masking its real potential, and then launches a surprise attack when the other jockeys are busy competing among themselves.

**Notable case:** In his 2011 Kentucky Derby victory with Animal Kingdom, Velazquez kept his horse out of the leading positions for most of the race, surprising everyone with a spectacular finish in the final stretch.

### 6. Jerry Bailey – "Constantly Changing Pace":
Jerry Bailey was a master at changing pace during races, tricking other jockeys into thinking his horse was either slowing down or speeding up at unexpected moments. This constant change in rhythm confused his rivals and made it difficult for them to plan their own attack.

**Notable case:** In the 2001 Breeders' Cup Classic with Tiznow, Bailey used this tactic to keep his rivals off their ideal pace and launched a final attack in the last stretch, winning the race for the second consecutive time.

### 7. Ryan Moore – "Controlling the Pack from the Front":
British jockey Ryan Moore is known for his ability to control the race while leading from the front. Often, Moore positions himself in the lead and sets a slow pace to prevent other horses from overtaking prematurely. The other jockeys, frustrated by trying to keep up with his controlled rhythm, find themselves caught off guard when Moore suddenly accelerates and launches his final attack.

**Notable case:** In the 2010 Epsom Derby with Workforce, Moore maintained a controlled pace for most of the race before launching a devastating attack in the final meters, winning by a large margin.

### 8. Angel Cordero Jr. – "Closing Gaps":
Puerto Rican jockey Angel Cordero Jr. was known for his aggressive tactic of closing gaps. Cordero not only ran his own race but also made it difficult for his rivals to advance by blocking the spaces they needed to overtake. This tactic intimidated other jockeys, forcing them to change their strategy or even slow down.

**Notable case:** Cordero used this tactic on numerous occasions throughout his career, and his ability to block his rivals was key to many of his victories, including his three Kentucky Derby wins.

### 9. Willie Shoemaker – "Feigning a Bad Start":

Willie Shoemaker, one of the legends of horse racing, was famous for his ability to feign a bad start. Shoemaker would let his horse appear to fall behind at the start of the race, leading other jockeys to believe that his horse wasn't in top form. However, when the rivals least expected it, Shoemaker would launch an attack from the back, quickly gaining positions.

**Notable case:** Shoemaker used this tactic with great success in the 1957 Belmont Stakes, when many thought he had no chance, but his impressive finish led him to win the race.

### 10. Victor Espinoza – "Psychological Distraction":

Victor Espinoza, known for winning the Triple Crown with American Pharoah in 2015, has employed subtler tactics, such as psychological distraction. Espinoza is known for studying the weaknesses of rival jockeys and exploiting them. Sometimes, his strategy involves mentally pressuring other jockeys, causing them to second-guess their own tactics, leading to mistakes.

**Notable case:** In the 2015 Kentucky Derby, many jockeys tried to keep up with American Pharoah's pace, but Espinoza maintained full control of the race, causing the other jockeys to burn their energy too early, allowing his horse to win comfortably.

# 33

**The longest horse race in the world is the Mongol Derby, an extreme endurance competition held annually in Mongolia.**

This race is recognized by the Guinness World Records as the longest horse race, covering a distance of approximately 1,000 kilometers (621 miles).

The Mongol Derby is inspired by the ancient messenger system used by the Mongol Empire under the rule of Genghis Khan in the 13th century, when riders traveled vast distances to deliver messages across the empire's extensive communication network.

The race is organized based on the model of the horse relay station system used by the Mongol empire.

Competitors ride a series of semi-wild Mongolian horses and change mounts every 40 kilometers (about 25 miles) at a series of stations known as urtuus.

This is similar to the historic system, where messengers would also switch horses to maintain a fast pace and ensure the horses did not become exhausted.

The terrain covered by the race varies greatly, including open steppes, mountains, deserts, and rivers, making the race incredibly challenging for both horses and riders.

Competitors must navigate on their own, using maps and GPS technology, and often face extreme weather conditions, ranging from scorching heat to torrential rain.

One of the most challenging aspects of the Mongol Derby is handling the Mongolian horses, which are small but extremely tough.

Although known for their strength and endurance, these horses can also be temperamental and difficult to control due to their semi-wild nature.

Riders must quickly establish a connection with each horse they ride in order to make progress in the race.

While the maximum time allowed to complete the race is 10 days, the best riders typically finish it in 7-8 days, depending on weather conditions and the terrain.

Riders must be self-sufficient during the race, carrying essentials such as food, water, and basic survival gear, as the terrain can be dangerous and the support stations are spaced far apart.

A crucial factor is that competitors must ensure the horses remain in good condition.

At each station, the horses are checked by veterinarians to make sure they are not overexerted.

If a horse shows signs of exhaustion or mistreatment, the rider may be penalized with time deductions or even disqualified.

Participants in the Mongol Derby come from all over the world and are typically experienced riders, as the race requires advanced horsemanship skills and physical endurance.

Competitors need to be not only skilled riders but also have great physical and mental stamina to endure long hours in the saddle, harsh weather conditions, and a lack of comforts.

In addition to professional riders, amateurs who train specifically for this event also participate.

The Mongol Derby is known for its level of difficulty and the numerous risks involved.

Riders may face injuries, from falls to extreme exhaustion. Some have been thrown from their horses or have gotten lost in the vast Mongolian plains.

The weather and terrain are unpredictable factors that can make the challenge even more daunting.

Despite the presence of medical personnel and veterinarians along the route, the race pushes participants to their physical and mental limits.

The Mongol Derby is not only one of the most extreme and demanding races in the world, but also one of the most unique, due to its historical connection with the Mongol past and Mongolia's equestrian culture.

The event offers riders an unforgettable experience, as they not only face the physical challenge of the race but also have the opportunity to immerse themselves in the nomadic culture and the breathtaking landscape of Mongolia.

Over the years, the Mongol Derby has gained popularity among adventurous riders and has attracted international media attention due to its reputation as the ultimate equestrian race.

The competition has been featured in documentaries and praised by those seeking an extraordinary challenge in the world of horse racing.

# 34

**Daily training of a professional jockey.**

**1. Exercise and Weight Control:** One of the most critical aspects for a jockey is maintaining their body weight within the required limits. For many jockeys, weight control is a constant challenge, as they need to stay light but strong enough to manage the horses. Jockeys typically weigh between 48 and 50 kg, and maintaining this weight often requires a strict diet and continuous physical training. The training day often begins early in the morning with light cardiovascular exercises such as running, cycling, or swimming, which help burn calories and keep them in shape without developing too much muscle mass. Additionally, many jockeys practice yoga or Pilates, as these exercises not only help keep their weight in check but also improve flexibility and posture, which are essential for riding.

**2. Core Strength and Endurance:** Although jockeys need to be light, they must also have a strong core to maintain balance and control over the horse. Core strength is essential because jockeys spend much of the race in a semi-squatting position and need to resist the forces of the horse's movement while maintaining stability. To strengthen their core, jockeys perform specific exercises such as sit-ups, planks, and light weight lifting. However, the weights they lift are usually moderate, as their main goal is to build strength without gaining too much size. In addition to core exercises, they also practice leg and arm exercises, as these muscles are crucial for giving precise cues to the horse during the race.

**3. Training on Riding Simulators:** Many professional

jockeys use horse simulators to train at home or in stables. These simulators mimic the movement of a racehorse and allow jockeys to work on their balance, riding position, and endurance without the need to ride a real horse. Simulators enable jockeys to practice riding techniques, such as the use of the whip and rein handling, improving their technique without the risk of injury.

**4. Riding on the Track:** A large part of a professional jockey's day is spent riding horses on the training track. Typically, jockeys work directly with trainers and owners to ride horses that are being prepared for upcoming races. These training sessions allow jockeys to become amiliar with each horse, understand their strengths and weaknesses, and adjust their race strategies accordingly. Jockeys often ride multiple horses throughout the day, as they need to adapt their riding style to different horses. During these training sessions, they practice race pacing, work on how to position the horse on the track, and improve their connection with the animal. It is during this phase that jockeys and horses develop a key relationship that will be essential for competitions.

**5. Studying Race Strategies:** In addition to physical training, a professional jockey spends time studying races. This includes reviewing footage of their past races to identify areas for improvement and analyzing their rivals' races. Many jockeys take time to study the riding styles of other jockeys and the tactics employed by competing horses. Study also includes analyzing track conditions, as different surfaces (dirt, turf, mud) may require different tactical approaches. A jockey needs to be fully informed about the condition of the track on which they will compete to make the necessary adjustments.

**6. Diet and Nutrition:** To control their weight and maintain a balanced diet, professional jockeys follow very strict meal plans. Their diet typically includes low-calorie but nutrient-rich foods such as fruits, vegetables, lean proteins (chicken, fish), and complex carbohydrates. Some jockeys also incorporate supplements to ensure they receive enough essential vitamins and minerals, as caloric restrictions may lead to nutrient deficiencies in their diet. Weight control is so important that some jockeys also use sauna sessions or hot baths to sweat and lose weight right before a race if they are slightly over their weight limit.

**7. Mental Training:** Mental training is another crucial part of a jockey's daily routine. Horse racing is mentally exhausting, as jockeys must make quick decisions on the track, adjust to the horse's movements, and react to changes in the position of competitors. Many jockeys work with sports psychologists to improve their focus, stress management, and confidence, especially before major races. Mental training also includes the ability to stay calm in difficult situations, such as when the horse is not responding as expected or when surrounded by other horses on the track.

**8. Rest and Recovery Sessions:** Given the high physical and mental demands, jockeys also dedicate time to recovery. This includes regular massages, stretching, and, in some cases, physical therapy to cope with the physical strain. Rest sessions are essential to prevent burnout and allow the body to recover from the daily demands.

# 35

**The term "Triple Crown" in horse racing refers to the ultimate achievement of a horse winning the three major races for three-year-old thoroughbreds in the United States: the Kentucky Derby, the Preakness Stakes, and the Belmont Stakes.**

Although this set of races has been regarded as the greatest challenge in horse racing since the early 20th century, the term "Triple Crown" was not officially coined until 1930.

It was in that year that sports journalist Charles Hatton, who worked for the "Daily Racing Form", began using the term to describe the feat accomplished by the horse Gallant Fox, who won all three prestigious races that same year.

Before 1930, while the three races were already held and recognized as important events on the racing calendar, there was no formal term to describe the achievement of winning all three.

The Kentucky Derby is the oldest of the three, first held in 1875 at Churchill Downs in Louisville, Kentucky.

The Preakness Stakes debuted in 1873 at Pimlico Race Course in Baltimore, Maryland, and the Belmont Stakes, the longest of the three races, was first held in 1867 in New York.

However, it wasn't until the early 20th century that the three races began to be considered a special trio, partly due to their growing popularity and increased media coverage.

The term "Triple Crown" began gaining popularity after 1930, as more horses attempted the feat of winning all three races.

Since Gallant Fox achieved this triumph, only a small number of horses have managed to win all three, making the Triple Crown one of the most prestigious and difficult accomplishments in equestrian sports.

Since its coining, only 13 horses have won the Triple Crown, the most recent being Justify in 2018.

Other famous winners include Secretariat in 1973, Seattle Slew in 1977, and American Pharoah in 2015, who ended a 37-year drought without a Triple Crown winner.

The distance and timing between the races are what make this achievement so difficult.

The Kentucky Derby is run over a mile and a quarter (2.01 km), the Preakness Stakes over a mile and three sixteenths (1.9 km), and the Belmont Stakes, the longest race, over a mile and a half (2.4 km).

The short recovery time between the Derby and the Preakness, and then between the Preakness and the Belmont, requires horses to have a combination of exceptional speed, stamina, and recovery ability to succeed.

The use of the term "Triple Crown" in the United States also inspired its adoption in other countries, such as in England, where it is used to describe the feat of winning the country's three classic races: the 2,000 Guineas, the Epsom Derby, and the St. Leger Stakes.

# 36

**The horse Reckless is known for being the oldest racehorse to actively compete, having raced until the remarkable age of 18, which is extremely unusual in the world of horse racing.**

In this sport, horses generally begin their racing careers around the age of two or three and typically retire between the ages of 7 and 8 due to the physical demands of competition.

Reckless' competitive longevity is particularly notable, as most racehorses experience a decline in performance long before reaching old age.

Racehorses usually retire earlier due to the physical stress they endure on their legs and joints, as the constant impact on the tracks can lead to injuries or progressive wear and tear on tendons and muscles.

However, Reckless was an exception.

His endurance and ability to stay fit at such an advanced age made him stand out in a sport where older horses are often relegated to breeding or retired to quieter pastures.

This is even more impressive when considering that older horses are more prone to joint or ligament issues, making his extended racing career quite an accomplishment.

It is unknown whether Reckless suffered any major injuries during his career, but it is certain that his trainer and team must have paid special attention to his physical care, maintaining a rigorous program of upkeep and rehabilitation to keep him competing.

Reckless' longevity likely also stems from superior genetics, with endurance and bone structure that allowed him to continue competing healthily beyond the usual timeframe.

Reckless' case is one of those standout examples in horse racing history, showing that, on rare occasions, some horses can defy expectations and extend their careers well beyond the average.

Reckless' extended career also sparked discussions about the health and well-being of racehorses, as staying competitive at an advanced age requires a careful balance between training and rest.

Today, it is rare to see older horses on the racetrack, as trainers typically prioritize preserving the horse's health for breeding or a peaceful retirement, but Reckless' story remains a reminder that, in certain cases, horses can remain strong and competitive for much longer.

Nowadays, most racehorses retire young to maximize their value in the breeding industry.

Horses that have been successful on the track are particularly valuable as breeding stock, as owners seek to pass on the winning traits of the parents to the next generation of racers.

# 37

**The use of silks, or distinctive colors in horse racing, has its roots in the Middle Ages, when they were used in knightly tournaments.**

During those tournaments, knights carried banners and colors that represented their lineage or family symbols, allowing spectators and opponents to easily identify participants during the competitions.

This visual identification system was crucial in a time when armor covered the faces and bodies of knights, making colors essential to distinguish who was who on the battlefield or in jousting events.

Over time, this tradition was adopted by the world of horse racing, which emerged in Europe as an extension of knighthood and equestrian sports.

Horse owners began using specific colors to make their animals easily identifiable on the racetrack.

Instead of representing knights or lineages, the silks represented the horse owners, and jockeys began wearing these colors on their jackets, caps, and equipment.

This development allowed spectators, judges, and other competitors to quickly recognize which horse belonged to each owner during a race.

The use of distinctive colors also became necessary for practical reasons.

In the early races, with crowds of horses and jockeys

competing at the same time, it was difficult for spectators, trainers, and officials to track the progress of a specific horse.

By incorporating colors, each horse and its jockey became easily identifiable from a distance, making the competition more accessible and exciting for the audience.

In the 18th century, when horse racing began to gain popularity in England, especially in places like Newmarket, the tradition of silks was formalized.

Rules were established to register the owners' colors, ensuring that each owner had a unique set of silks, thereby avoiding confusion among the participants.

This also allowed owners to express their personality and status through the design of their silks' colors and patterns, becoming a visual extension of their identity in the competition.

Over the centuries, the colors and designs of silks have evolved.

Although they were originally simple and represented noble families, over time they have become more creative and varied, adopting a wide range of color combinations and patterns.

Stripes, checks, diamonds, stars, and other graphic designs now adorn silks, making the races even more visually striking.

Despite this evolution, the basic function remains the same: to identify the horse's owner and make the competitors visible during the race.

Today, silks remain an important symbol in horse racing, and each owner must register their colors with the relevant racing authority, such as the Jockey Club in the United Kingdom or various equestrian organizations in other countries.

These registrations ensure that each set of colors is unique.

Additionally, some colors or combinations have become iconic due to their association with champion horses or legendary owners.

For example, the famous green and pink silks of Juddmonte Farms, owned by Khalid Abdullah, have been associated with some of the most successful horses in history.

# 38

**The shortest horse race in the world is run in France, at the famous Auteuil racecourse in Paris, and covers a distance of only 350 meters.**

Auteuil is mainly known for its obstacle races and its significance in the French horse racing calendar, but this short and explosive race, unique in its kind, has captured the attention of fans due to its uniqueness.

Unlike traditional horse races, which usually range between 1,200 and 2,400 meters, this 350-meter race is an extreme test of pure speed and explosiveness for both horses and jockeys.

In these short races, which can last only a few seconds, the horses must maximize their acceleration and maintain top speed from the start, making race strategy completely different from longer races, where endurance and pace management play an important role.

These short races require a particular type of training for both the horse and the jockey.

Instead of focusing on endurance, trainers prepare the horses to have a quick start and a sustained burst of speed over the brief distance of the race.

The horses competing in this type of race are usually thoroughbreds specifically selected for their ability to reach maximum speed in a very short amount of time.

In addition to pure speed, the jockey's reflexes and ability to make quick decisions at the start are crucial in a race of such short distance.

In longer races, jockeys have time to adjust their strategies based on the performance of other competitors, but in a 350-meter race, any mistake at the start or in the first few meters can be fatal, as there is not enough time to recover from a bad start.

These short races are also known for their spectacle and the speed with which they unfold.

For spectators, the experience is completely different, as instead of following the progress of the horses along a longer track, the focus is on the first few seconds and the horses' ability to accelerate to maximum speed right from the start.

Auteuil is one of the most iconic racecourses in France, famous for hosting some of the most important steeplechase races in the world, such as the Grand Steeple-Chase de Paris.

However, this pure speed race is an exception within the usual programming of the racecourse, making it even more attractive and exciting for fans looking for something out of the ordinary.

Although this short race does not have the same level of prestige as events like the Prix de l'Arc de Triomphe or the major steeplechase races, it remains a notable competition in the horse racing scene, as it challenges both horses and jockeys in a unique way.

# 39

**The fastest horse ever recorded was a thoroughbred named Winning Brew, who reached an astounding speed of 70.76 km/h (43.97 mph) during a race in 2008.**

This record was certified by the Guinness Book of World Records and took place at Penn National Race Course in Pennsylvania, United States.

Winning Brew, trained by Francis Vitale, achieved this feat in a short-distance race of two furlongs (approximately 402 meters), a distance where horses can reach their maximum speed without needing to reserve energy for longer distances.

The impressive speed of Winning Brew stands out for several reasons.

In horse racing, reaching these speeds is extremely difficult due to the biomechanical and physiological challenges horses face.

In Winning Brew's case, her ability to reach and maintain this speed was due to a combination of factors such as her genetics, specialized training, and a race designed to maximize pure speed over a short distance.

Two-furlong races are tests where horses can focus solely on acceleration and explosive speed from the start, allowing them to reach much higher speeds than in longer races, like the Kentucky Derby or the Belmont Stakes, where endurance also plays a crucial role.

Winning Brew's record of 70.76 km/h is the result of exceptional equine biomechanics.

Thoroughbreds, known for being the dominant breed in horse racing, are genetically predisposed for speed due to their body structure, which allows for greater aerodynamic efficiency.

They have long, muscular legs, a highly developed cardiovascular system, and a unique ability to maximize oxygen flow to their muscles during extreme exertion.

These characteristics are essential for achieving high speeds in short-distance races.

Another key factor that contributed to this historic record was the rigorous training Winning Brew underwent.

Her trainer, Francis Vitale, meticulously worked on improving her explosiveness and acceleration, which was crucial for Winning Brew to reach her full potential on the track.

Training horses for short races is very different from training them for endurance races, as the horses must be able to reach their top speed within seconds of leaving the starting gate.

This involves a focus on speed, strength, and short-duration muscle endurance exercises, which allowed Winning Brew to excel in this test.

In addition to genetics and training, the track conditions where Winning Brew set her record were also an important factor.

Race tracks, whether they are made of grass, dirt, or synthetic materials, can influence the horse's traction and speed.

In Winning Brew's case, the surface of the Penn National track would have been carefully maintained to ensure optimal footing, allowing the horse to perform to its full potential without obstacles.

Winning Brew's record is an outstanding achievement in the history of horse racing and remains a global benchmark in terms of equine speed.

Although many thoroughbred horses are known for their speed and athletic ability, few have reached the velocity that Winning Brew achieved in 2008.

This record still stands as a testament to the incredible ability of thoroughbred horses to maximize their speed over short distances.

# 40

**In conditions of extreme heat or stress, it is common to observe some horses sweating a white foam, especially visible in areas like the base of the neck, the chest, and between the legs.**

This phenomenon occurs due to a combination of physiological factors related to horse sweat and how their body handles heat stress.

Horse sweat contains a protein called latherin, which acts as a surfactant.

When horses sweat heavily, especially during intense exercise or in hot conditions, the continuous movement of their muscles and the natural agitation of the sweat cause the latherin in the sweat to mix with the air, creating a white foam.

This foam is more visible in areas where there is more muscle movement, such as the neck or legs, and where sweat tends to accumulate.

This type of sweating is a natural mechanism for horses to regulate their body temperature.

Horses are large animals that generate a considerable amount of heat during exercise or in hot climates.

Sweating helps dissipate this excess heat, but in certain conditions, especially when humidity is high or the horse is under great physical exertion, the sweating process can become more extreme, resulting in the formation of foam.

Often, white foam is an indication that the horse is working very hard or is under significant heat, and it is a sign of exertion.

However, while sweating foam is not necessarily dangerous, it is important to monitor horses when this occurs, as it may be an indication that they are reaching their physical limit.

Horses can become dehydrated quickly in extreme heat or during intense races, which can lead to exhaustion or even more serious health issues, such as heatstroke.

It is essential to provide them with water and allow them to rest in these situations so they can recover properly.

Sweat evaporation is one of the primary ways horses cool their bodies, and when sweat turns to foam, it means the process is working correctly, but also that the horse is sweating in large amounts.

Trainers and caretakers typically pay attention to the amount of sweat and the physical signs of their horses to ensure they are not at risk of overheating.

# 41

**In horse racing, horse names are strictly regulated by various racing authorities worldwide, such as the Jockey Club in the United States and similar organizations in other countries.**

One of the main rules regarding names is that they cannot exceed 18 characters, including spaces and punctuation marks.

This character limit ensures that names can fit legibly on official forms, race bulletins, and result boards, as well as ensuring that names are easy to pronounce and remember.

In addition to the character restriction, there are also other rules governing the selection of horse names.

For example, names that have already been assigned to famous horses or Triple Crown winners are prohibited.

This is to preserve the legacy of historic horses and avoid confusion with new runners.

Similarly, names that may be considered offensive, include inappropriate references, or suggest a trademark are also prohibited.

Another important rule is that horse names cannot be identical or too similar to recently registered horses, to avoid confusion in race results and pedigree records.

Racing authorities maintain databases with thousands of registered names, and owners must review these lists to ensure their name choice is available.

Additionally, in some cases, names can be reused, but only if a significant amount of time has passed since the previous horse with that name stopped competing or passed away, and only if that horse did not have a particularly distinguished career.

The name registration process is considered a crucial step when a young horse is being prepared for its racing debut.

Owners often get creative during this process, trying to find names that have personal meaning, are related to the horse's lineage, or simply sound good and are easy to remember.

Some names reference the horse's parents, while others are wordplays or reflect some aspect of the horse's character or appearance.

# 42

**Just like people, some horses show a natural preference for turning left or right, making them "left-handed" or "right-handed" in terms of their movements on the track.**

This preference is related to their biomechanics, muscle coordination, and balance, which influence their ability to take turns smoothly and efficiently.

The preference for turning in a particular direction is not just a matter of training but also has biological roots, as some horses have one side of their body that is stronger or more flexible than the other.

This natural preference can affect a horse's performance on different types of tracks.

In the United States, most racetracks are designed for horses to run to the left (counterclockwise).

Horses that naturally prefer turning left (i.e., "left-handed") tend to perform better on these tracks, as they can take the turns more quickly without losing as much balance or speed.

On the other hand, horses that prefer turning to the right may struggle more on these tracks, as their natural movement does not align with left-hand turns.

In Great Britain, Australia, and other countries, some tracks allow races to be run to the right (clockwise), which benefits "right-handed" horses that naturally prefer turning right.

On these types of tracks, a horse that prefers to turn right may have an advantage when taking turns, maintaining better balance and less loss of speed compared to horses that prefer turning left.

Horse training can be adapted to improve performance on tracks that do not match their natural inclination.

Jockeys and trainers pay attention to these preferences and often train horses to perform better in both directions, though this can require extra effort and time.

Even so, many horses show better results on tracks that align with their natural tendency.

**Examples of famous horses and their preferences:**

**-Secretariat:** Considered one of the greatest racehorses in history, he had outstanding ability on both left-turning and right-turning tracks, making him virtually unbeatable. However, he excelled on U.S. tracks, where most races turn left.

**-Frankel:** Another of the most dominant horses of all time, he competed mainly in the United Kingdom, where some races are held on right-turning tracks. His ability to adapt to different types of tracks made him a legend.

**-American Pharoah:** The 2015 Triple Crown winner performed exceptionally well on U.S. tracks that turn left, which was a key advantage in his path to the Triple Crown, as all those races are run on left-turning tracks.

**-Winx:** The Australian mare who won 33 consecutive races also competed on several right-turning tracks. Her ability to adapt to that type of track made her unstoppable in her racing career in Australia.

**-Zenyatta:** A legendary mare in U.S. racing, Zenyatta had an impressive winning streak. Her natural preference was to turn left, which made her stand out on U.S. tracks, which generally turn in that direction.

**-Cigar:** Another famous horse in racing history, Cigar showed a strong preference for left-turning tracks. His performance on U.S. tracks made him a legend with a streak of 16 consecutive victories.

**-Phar Lap:** The famous Australian horse, although he excelled on both left- and right-turning tracks, showed a slight inclination for races on right-turning tracks, as seen on many Australian and New Zealand tracks.

**-Tiznow:** This horse, a consecutive winner of the Breeders' Cup Classic in 2000 and 2001, performed well on left-turning tracks, favored by his natural preference for this type of circuit in U.S. races.

**-Galileo:** This Irish horse, known for his success in longer-distance races, competed on European tracks, where races can turn both left and right. However, it was noted that he had greater maneuverability on right-turning tracks.

# 43

**Horses have an incredibly wide field of vision, almost 360 degrees, due to the lateral position of their eyes on the skull.**

This configuration gives them an evolutionary advantage, as they are prey animals and need to be alert to potential dangers in their environment.

This ability to see almost everything happening around them without having to turn their head allows them to quickly detect any nearby movement, which is essential for their survival in the wild.

Most of a horse's visual field is monocular, meaning each eye can see independently.

This allows them to perceive different images with each eye, covering almost every angle around their body.

However, there are two blind spots in their vision: one directly behind them and another right in front of their muzzle.

These areas are minimal compared to their overall visual field, but it is important to note that if an object or movement occurs in these blind spots, the horse will need to move its head to see it.

While their ability to see in nearly 360 degrees provides a significant advantage in terms of threat detection, it also has some disadvantages.

Horses do not have good depth perception in their

monocular vision, which can make it difficult for them to accurately judge the distance of objects they are observing with one eye.

To improve their depth perception, a horse needs to use both eyes and look directly in front of them, where they have a small area of binocular vision.

Additionally, their vision is adapted to better perceive quick movements around them, allowing them to react to potential predators or dangerous situations almost instantly.

This ability to detect even the subtlest changes in their environment explains why horses can easily startle at sudden movements that occur outside their direct field of vision.

# 44

**Horse racing on the beach is a unique and exciting tradition held in various parts of the world, particularly popular on the coast of Ireland, where horses race on wet sand instead of traditional turf or dirt tracks.**

These races take advantage of low tide, which creates a firm and relatively stable surface for the horses to run on.

This type of race offers an impressive visual spectacle and has become an attraction for both locals and tourists.

One of the most famous locations for these races is Laytown, a small coastal village on the east coast of Ireland.

The Laytown races are particularly unique because they are one of the few such competitions officially authorized by racing authorities and are held under official horse racing rules.

Each year, in September, during low tide, these races are organized on an expansive beach, and the horses race on wet sand, which is firmer and less treacherous than dry sand, allowing them to maintain good traction.

Racing on the beach presents different challenges for both horses and jockeys.

Although wet sand provides a firmer surface than dry sand, it is still less stable than a turf or dirt track.

Horses must adapt to the changing surface conditions, and jockeys must be especially attentive to variations in the sand to prevent their mounts from losing traction or tiring quickly.

Additionally, the salty air and proximity to the sea create a completely different environment compared to conventional tracks.

These races are often part of festivals or community events, and besides the races, attendees enjoy recreational activities, live music, and other forms of entertainment.

In Laytown, for example, the races have been an annual tradition for over a century, making them one of the oldest equestrian events in Ireland.

Beach races are not exclusive to Ireland.

In Spain, the beach of Sanlúcar de Barrameda, on the Andalusian coast, is also known for its horse races held during the summer.

These races, which take place from mid-August to early September, are a tradition dating back over 175 years and attract thousands of spectators each year.

In Sanlúcar, the horses race along the shoreline with the impressive backdrop of the Guadalquivir River and Doñana National Park.

Another famous location for beach races is Omaha Beach in Normandy, France, where horses compete on the historic beach in an event that combines history with the thrill of racing.

# 45

## The case of the "ghost jockey" is one of the most unusual and surprising events in the history of horse racing.

It occurred in 1923 during a race at Belmont Park in New York, when jockey Frank Hayes, riding a horse named Sweet Kiss, won the race after having passed away during the competition.

This incident became legendary in the racing world and was widely reported at the time due to its shocking nature.

Frank Hayes, who was 35 at the time, was not a professional jockey; in fact, he primarily worked as a trainer and stable hand.

On the day of the race, he was given the opportunity to ride Sweet Kiss, a horse that was not considered a favorite to win.

Hayes had worked with the horse for some time and prepared to compete in what would have been his first official victory as a jockey.

During the race, Sweet Kiss and Hayes surprised everyone by leading the competition and eventually crossing the finish line in first place.

However, shortly after the race, track staff and the other jockeys noticed that Hayes was not moving on the horse.

It was then discovered that, at some point during the race, Hayes had suffered a heart attack and passed away while still in the saddle.

Somehow, his body remained in position on the horse, and Sweet Kiss continued running and won the race.

The event was described by the press as the victory of the "ghost jockey," as Hayes technically won the race even after his death.

After the tragic discovery, the jockey was declared dead at the racetrack, and it is believed that the physical effort and stress of the race were the factors that triggered the heart attack.

This incident, in addition to its tragic nature, left a mark in racing history.

Sweet Kiss, the horse that carried Hayes to his unusual victory, never raced again.

According to some stories, the horse was given the nickname "Sweet Kiss of Death" due to the unusual and sad end to the race.

# 46

**The term "dark horse" originated in the world of horse racing and has since been widely used in other contexts to describe an unexpected or unknown competitor who surprises by winning or performing better than expected.**

In horse racing, a "dark horse" originally referred to a little-known runner, one that had been kept secret or had competed in very few races, so its true potential was unclear and unpredictable to bettors or the public.

This type of horse, which seemingly has little chance of winning due to its lack of track record or previous victories, can end up surprising everyone by winning the race, outperforming the more well-known favorites.

The term became popular due to the unexpected nature of such victories and has become a widely used metaphor for any situation where someone or something with no prior notoriety achieves significant success.

The use of the term can be traced back to at least the 19th century, when British writer Benjamin Disraeli used it in his novel The Young Duke (1831).

In the story, Disraeli describes a horse that no one expected to win, suddenly emerging to claim victory, surprising everyone present.

The concept of the "dark horse" is also closely related to betting.

In the world of horse racing betting, horses that are not

well-known or do not have a remarkable track record tend to have higher odds, as they are not expected to win.

However, if one of these unknown or long-shot horses surprises everyone and wins, both bettors and the public experience an unexpected twist.

Over time, the term has transcended the realm of horse racing and is used in a variety of situations, such as politics, sports, entertainment, and other fields.

In politics, for example, a "dark horse" can refer to a candidate who is not well-known but manages to win or achieve unexpected success in an election.

In sports, it is also used to describe teams or athletes who were not favorites to win but surprise with their performance.

# 47

**In long-distance or high-intensity horse races, horses can experience significant weight loss in a very short time, losing up to 20 kilograms of body weight due to sweating and physical exertion.**

This rapid weight loss occurs mainly due to dehydration, as horses sweat profusely during intense exercise, especially in hot conditions.

Being large, warm-blooded animals, horses generate a significant amount of body heat when they run.

To regulate their temperature and avoid overheating, they sweat in large amounts.

Through sweat, they not only lose water but also essential electrolytes like sodium, potassium, and chloride, which contributes to a rapid reduction in body weight.

In endurance races, where horses cover long distances that can exceed 80 or 100 kilometers, this weight loss is especially noticeable.

As the horse continues running, the need to cool its body and maintain its energy levels leads to a significant amount of water evaporating through sweat.

Although this weight loss is temporary and primarily caused by fluid loss, it can have a significant impact on the horse's performance and health if not properly managed.

After the race, it is crucial that the horse is rehydrated and receives proper care to recover the lost fluids and electrolytes.

Trainers often provide them with water, electrolyte drinks, or special solutions to help replenish what has been lost.

The rapid weight loss can also cause horses to tire more quickly or become more prone to cramps or exhaustion if not properly managed.

Despite this rapid weight loss during a race, most horses fully recover once they are given enough time to rest, rehydrate, and be properly fed.

However, this fluctuation in weight is one of the reasons why horses must be closely monitored during competitions, as excessive loss of fluids and electrolytes can have serious health consequences if not treated in time.

# 48

**The Saudi Cup is currently the horse race with the largest prize purse in the world, with an impressive sum of $20 million.**

This race has become the most lucrative in the world since its first edition in 2020 and has attracted the best horses, jockeys, and trainers from around the globe due to the enormous financial incentives it offers.

Of the $20 million, $10 million is awarded to the winner, making it one of the most coveted competitions on the international horse racing calendar.

Held at the King Abdulaziz Racetrack in Riyadh, Saudi Arabia, the Saudi Cup is a dirt race, run over a distance of 1,800 meters (approximately 9 furlongs), placing it in the mid-range in terms of race length.

The race is designed to attract the best horses from around the world, including those that have competed in prestigious events like the Kentucky Derby, the Dubai World Cup, and the Breeders' Cup Classic.

The launch of the Saudi Cup was a significant move in the horse racing industry, which has historically seen some of the largest purses in competitions like the Dubai World Cup (with a $12 million purse before the Saudi Cup) and the Pegasus World Cup in the United States.

The creation of this race not only increased global competition but also established Saudi Arabia as a new hub for elite horse racing competitions.

The financial significance of the Saudi Cup has revolutionized the sport, offering unprecedented opportunities for owners, trainers, and jockeys to earn significant profits.

At the same time, the race has allowed Saudi Arabia to boost its reputation in the world of horse racing, competing directly with other major events in the United Arab Emirates, the United States, the United Kingdom, and France.

In addition to the enormous prize purse, the Saudi Cup has also drawn attention due to its top-tier organization and the impressive facilities at the King Abdulaziz Racetrack, designed to accommodate thousands of spectators and provide a world-class experience for participants.

Despite its recent inception, the Saudi Cup has already established itself as one of the most prestigious and anticipated events on the horse racing calendar.

# 49

**Just like runners who use specialized footwear, racehorses also wear special horseshoes designed to improve their traction and performance on different types of tracks.**

These horseshoes not only protect their hooves but are also adapted to the surface conditions on which they compete, helping to maximize their speed and stability during the race.

Racehorse shoes are made from lightweight materials such as aluminum, which is significantly lighter than the traditional iron horseshoes used in other equestrian disciplines.

The lighter weight reduces the load on the horse's legs, allowing them to run faster and with greater agility.

Additionally, the shoes are designed to provide maximum traction on different track surfaces, whether dirt, turf, or synthetic surfaces.

Each type of track requires specific adaptations in the shoes for the horses to perform optimally:

**-Dirt tracks:** Races on dirt tracks, such as those common in the United States, require shoes that provide good traction without being too heavy. Some of these shoes may include small studs or cleats that help horses maintain their stability while running on dirt, especially in wet or muddy conditions.

**-Turf tracks:** On turf tracks, commonly found in Europe

and some other countries, horseshoes are also designed to improve grip on a surface that can be slippery due to wet grass. Removable studs are sometimes used in the shoes to provide better traction on soft or wet ground.

**-Synthetic tracks:** In racetracks that use synthetic surfaces, the horseshoes are adapted to provide a balance between traction and comfort, as these surfaces are usually more consistent and softer than dirt or turf tracks. Shoes designed for synthetic tracks may have less need for additional studs or cleats.

In addition to traction, horseshoes are also designed to protect the horse's hooves, which are susceptible to injury due to the repeated impact with the track.

Without proper horseshoes, racehorses would be more prone to hoof damage, which could affect their performance or, in the worst case, lead to injuries that take them out of competition.

The farrier, the person responsible for fitting horseshoes to horses, plays a crucial role in the horse's performance.

Farriers specializing in racehorses work closely with trainers and veterinarians to ensure that each horse has the appropriate shoes based on their running style, track surface, and the weather conditions on race day.

# 50

**In horse racing, the term "dead weight" refers to the additional weight that jockeys must add to the saddle to meet the weight requirements set for the race.**

Each race has an assigned weight category, which specifies the total weight the horse must carry, including the jockey, the saddle, and any additional weight needed to reach the minimum or maximum required weight.

If the jockey and the equipment weigh less than required, "dead weight" is added in the form of ballast.

The purpose of these weight requirements is to ensure greater fairness in competitions, preventing lighter horses or jockeys from having an unfair advantage.

Therefore, if a jockey weighs less than the stipulated amount for the race, ballast is added to the saddle to compensate for the difference and meet the regulatory weight.

"Dead weight" is usually added in the form of lead or heavy material bags placed inside special pockets or compartments in the saddle.

These additional weights are distributed in such a way that they do not negatively affect the horse's balance or the jockey's comfort during the race.

The use of "dead weight" can be a challenge for jockeys and trainers, as the weight distribution must be carefully calculated to avoid interfering with the horse's performance.

Although the additional weight is inert (hence the term "dead weight"), it can still influence the horse's agility and speed.

However, unlike the jockey's weight, which can move during the race, the dead weight remains static and does not change the jockey's dynamics on the horse.

Weight requirements in races vary depending on the type of race, category, and the horse's age, among other factors.

In some elite competitions, such as the Kentucky Derby, the assigned weights can be very strict, and jockeys must ensure they meet these exact requirements.

Jockeys are typically short in stature and lightweight, but even so, they often need to add dead weight to reach the necessary minimum.

The balance between the jockey's weight and the dead weight is crucial for race performance, and any mistake in weight distribution can affect the horse's stability in turns or during the final stretches of the race.

For this reason, trainers, jockeys, and farriers work together to ensure that the weight is correctly distributed and does not interfere with the horse's natural running form.

# 51

**In the 1940s, an unusual and surprising incident occurred in the world of horse racing when a horse named Midnight Sun made history by running "headless," meaning without visible control from the jockey.**

During the race, Midnight Sun lost part of his bridle, the essential equipment that allows the jockey to guide and control the horse.

Without this bridle, the horse appeared to be running without the jockey having control over its direction or speed, leading to the race being described as if the horse was running "headless."

Despite the loss of the bridle, which is a key component for steering the horse during the race, Midnight Sun continued running with determination and in an extraordinary manner.

Amazingly, he managed to maintain the proper pace and direction to complete the race.

Although he did not win, Midnight Sun crossed the finish line in an incredible second place, which was considered a remarkable achievement given that he was running without the jockey's usual guidance.

The fact that Midnight Sun managed to finish the race in such a high position without the jockey's control demonstrates the incredible muscle memory and instinct of racehorses, which, in extreme situations, seem to continue running simply due to their prior training and natural competitive drive.

Although jockeys play a crucial role in guiding the horse, this incident highlighted that well-trained horses have the ability to maintain their focus and speed even in adverse circumstances.

The incident with Midnight Sun has become a legendary anecdote in the history of the sport, not only because of the unusual fact of running without a bridle but also for the horse's ability to achieve such a remarkable result without the usual intervention of his jockey.

This event reflects the determination and athletic ability of racehorses, which are capable of quickly adapting to unexpected situations and continuing to compete at a high level.

These types of episodes also highlight the risks faced by both horses and jockeys in horse racing, where any issue with equipment, such as the loss of a bridle or stirrup, can jeopardize control and safety during the race.

Nevertheless, the story of Midnight Sun remains remembered as an example of the incredible ability of horses to excel even in the most challenging circumstances.

# 52

**Horses can run smoothly under artificial lights, which has allowed some races to take place at night in various parts of the world.**

One of the most iconic venues where night races are held is the Happy Valley Racecourse in Hong Kong.

This racecourse is famous for its night races, which are held under powerful lights that illuminate the entire track, creating a spectacular atmosphere for both competitors and spectators.

Night races at Happy Valley have gained great popularity not only among local fans but also among tourists.

The track is surrounded by tall buildings and city lights, giving it a unique and vibrant atmosphere.

The use of artificial lights allows races to be held at times more convenient for spectators, and in many cases, it aims to attract a broader audience, as night races offer a different experience from traditional daytime races.

The performance of horses under artificial lights is not affected, as these lights are designed to be bright enough to replicate daylight and prevent visibility issues.

Additionally, horses are animals with good vision in low-light conditions, allowing them to quickly adapt to the conditions of night races.

The lights at racecourses are strategically arranged to eliminate shadows that could distract or disorient horses and jockeys while competing.

In addition to Happy Valley, other famous racecourses around the world have also adopted the night race format, such as Meydan Racecourse in Dubai and Moonee Valley Racecourse in Australia.

These events have become increasingly common due to their commercial appeal and the opportunity to offer races at more flexible times.

Night races also have the advantage of offering a cooler environment, especially in places with hot climates, which can be less exhausting for the horses compared to races held during the heat of the day.

However, both trainers and organizers must ensure that the lighting conditions are adequate and safe to guarantee the horses' well-being and the smooth running of the race.

# 53

**In various regions of the Middle East, camel racing is a deeply rooted tradition and is as popular as horse racing in other parts of the world.**

These races, especially in countries like the United Arab Emirates, Qatar, Saudi Arabia, and Oman, attract thousands of spectators and are considered a traditional and culturally significant sport.

Camels are iconic animals in these regions, known for their endurance in the desert, which makes them ideal competitors for this type of event.

One of the most interesting and technologically advanced features of modern camel racing is the use of robot jockeys.

These robotic jockeys have replaced human jockeys, especially children who used to ride them, due to concerns about human rights and the safety of children in this sport.

The robot jockeys, controlled remotely, allow the camels to be guided during the race without putting a person at risk.

These robot jockeys are lightweight, compact devices placed on the camel's hump.

They are equipped with levers that control the camel's reins and with mechanical whips that can be remotely activated to encourage the camel to speed up.

The trainers and owners of the camels follow the race from vehicles driving alongside the track, controlling the robot jockey via remote controls.

They also use microphones to give instructions to the camels, which are trained to respond to their trainers' voices.

Camel races are usually held on long sand tracks that can vary between 4 and 10 kilometers in length.

Camels, known for their ability to run long distances at a good pace, are rigorously trained to maximize their performance in these competitions.

The races often attract large crowds, and, much like horse racing, there are large cash prizes and prestige for the winners.

The introduction of robot jockeys has modernized the sport and allowed the tradition of camel racing to continue while addressing concerns about the welfare of human jockeys, especially children, who were often used in the past.

Robots are also more efficient and are not affected by desert conditions, such as extreme heat, ensuring more consistent performance in the races.

# 54

**In many horse races, even horses that do not win or finish in the top positions can receive a monetary prize simply for participating.**

This type of prize structure, known as a participation prize or "pay-for-play," is designed to help horse owners cover the costs of training and other expenses associated with preparing a racehorse.

The costs of maintaining and training a racehorse are high.

From feeding and veterinary care to the salaries of trainers, farriers, jockeys, and other team members, each race involves a significant investment.

In this context, the participation prize serves as an incentive for more owners to compete, even if their horses are not favorites to win.

The amount that non-winning horses receive varies depending on the race, the type of event, and the level of competition.

In some high-profile races, horses finishing in lower positions can still receive a substantial portion of the total prize money.

In lower-level races, participation prizes tend to be more modest, but they still help cover some of the expenses.

Typically, in group or elite races, prizes are distributed beyond first place, rewarding horses that finish in the top 5 or top 6.

However, in some competitions, all the horses entered may receive a small amount just for being present and competing in the race.

This practice is common at racetracks where the goal is to maintain healthy competition and encourage more owners to enter their horses.

The tiered prize system also encourages greater participation, as it not only rewards the winners but also the horses that show effort, allowing owners to continue investing in improving their horses and competing in future races.

In some cases, participation prizes also cover the entry fee for the race, which can be substantial in certain high-profile events.

# 55

**The story of Seattle Slew, one of the most legendary horses in racing history, is fascinating not only because of his success on the track but also due to his surprising origins.**

Although there is a common misconception about his price, the figure of 16 dollars is not entirely accurate.

Seattle Slew was purchased for $17,500 at an auction in 1975, which, while a considerable sum, was relatively low compared to other high-quality thoroughbred colts that often sell for much more.

Seattle Slew did not come from a prestigious line nor had the most desirable pedigree, which led his buyers, Karen and Mickey Taylor and Jim and Sally Hill, to acquire him at that price.

Despite his modest beginnings, Seattle Slew made racing history by becoming the only horse to win the Triple Crown (Kentucky Derby, Preakness Stakes, and Belmont Stakes) while remaining undefeated in all competitions up to that point.

His feat in 1977 cemented him as one of the greatest horses of all time.

Seattle Slew not only won the Triple Crown but also had an incredibly successful career as a sire, leaving a profound mark on the genetics of horse racing.

Throughout his career, he accumulated over $1.2 million in prize money and became an extremely influential stallion, producing multiple champions who perpetuated his legacy.

The contrast between the price he was bought for at auction and his subsequent success highlights one of the most exciting and unpredictable aspects of the horse racing world: a horse without an impressive pedigree or an exorbitant auction price can, with the right training and care, become a true legend.

Seattle Slew is an iconic example of how horse racing can be full of surprises, where a colt's value is not always reflected in its initial price, but in its ability to surprise on the track and write its own legacy in the history of the turf.

# 56

**In the 2007 Dubai World Cup, one of the most
prestigious events in the world of horse racing,
one of the closest and most dramatic finishes
in the sport's history occurred.**

The race took place at the Meydan Racecourse in Dubai, and the finish was so tight that it required a photo review lasting more than 20 minutes to determine the winner.

This event left a mark in the history of horse racing not only because of the intensity of the competition but also due to the enormous uncertainty surrounding the final result.

The two horses at the center of this close finish were Invasor, an Argentine thoroughbred, and Premium Tap, who fought head-to-head to the finish line.

Tension grew as both horses crossed the finish line almost simultaneously, making it impossible for the judges to immediately declare a winner.

Since the margin of victory was imperceptible to the naked eye, race officials turned to photo finish technology to determine which of the two horses had won the Dubai World Cup.

The review process took longer than usual, as the margin was so small that the images had to be carefully examined to ensure the correct decision was made.

Finally, after more than 20 minutes of analysis, it was determined that the winner was Invasor, by an extremely narrow margin.

Invasor, trained by Kiaran McLaughlin and ridden by jockey Fernando Jara, cemented his status as one of the greatest horses of his generation with this victory.

The 2007 Dubai World Cup was the last major triumph in Invasor's brilliant career, having previously won the Breeders' Cup Classic in 2006 and being named Horse of the Year in the United States.

This incredibly close finish and the prolonged photo review process highlighted the precision and modern technology required in horse racing, where fractions of a second can make the difference between glory and second place.